New Directions for Student Services

John H. Schuh
EDITOR-IN-CHIEF

Elizabeth J. Whitt
ASSOCIATE EDITOR

Creating a Veteran-Friendly Campus: Strategies for Transition and Success

Robert Ackerman
David DiRamio
EDITORS

Number 126 • Summer 2009
Jossey-Bass
San Francisco

CREATING A VETERAN-FRIENDLY CAMPUS: STRATEGIES FOR TRANSITION
AND SUCCESS
Robert Ackerman, David DiRamio (eds.)
New Directions for Student Services, no. 126
John H. Schuh, Editor-in-Chief
Elizabeth J. Whitt, Associate Editor

NEW DIRECTIONS FOR STUDENT SERVICES (ISSN 0164-7970, e-ISSN 1536-
0695) is part of The Jossey-Bass Higher and Adult Education Series and
is published quarterly by Wiley Subscription Services, Inc., A Wiley Com-
pany, at Jossey-Bass, 989 Market Street, San Francisco, California 94103-
1741. Periodicals Postage Paid at San Francisco, California, and at
additional mailing offices. POSTMASTER: Send address changes to New
Directions for Student Services, Jossey-Bass, 989 Market Street, San Francisco, CA 94103-1741.

New Directions for Student Services is indexed in CIJE: Current Index to
Journals in Education (ERIC), Contents Pages in Education (T&F),
Current Abstracts (EBSCO), Education Index/Abstracts (H.W. Wilson),
Educational Research Abstracts Online (T&F), ERIC Database (Educa-
tion Resources Information Center), and Higher Education Abstracts
(Claremont Graduate University).

Microfilm copies of issues and articles are available in 16mm and 35mm,
as well as microfiche in 105mm, through University Microfilms Inc., 300
North Zeeb Road, Ann Arbor, Michigan 48106-1346.

SUBSCRIPTIONS cost $98 for individuals and $251 for institutions, agencies,
and libraries in the United States.

EDITORIAL CORRESPONDENCE should be sent to the Editor-in-Chief, John
H. Schuh, N 243 Lagomarcino Hall, Iowa State University, Ames, Iowa
50011.

www.josseybass.com

CONTENTS

EDITORS' NOTES 1
Robert Ackerman, David DiRamio

1. Transitions: Combat Veterans as College Students 5
Robert Ackerman, David DiRamio, Regina L. Garza Mitchell
This chapter presents research on how students have handled the transition from combat to campus and uses these personal experiences to shape recommendations on how campuses can address the special needs of this population.

2. The Mobilization and Return of Undergraduate Students 15
Serving in the National Guard and Reserves
Mark Bauman
Personnel in the National Guard and reserves are subjected to periodic activations that are disruptive to their enrollment as students. This chapter reports on research that explains the transitions that students go through when they are called to active duty and later return to student status.

3. Supporting Student Veterans in Transition 25
Corey B. Rumann, Florence A. Hamrick
Relationships between higher education and the military to support students who are veterans have developed over time. This chapter examines how the changing needs of the military have influenced the development of campus-based programs to meet the needs of veterans.

4. Meeting the Needs of Women Veterans 35
Margaret Baechtold, Danielle M. De Sawal
The conflicts in the Middle East have changed the role of women in the military, and the impact of the changes are not fully understood. This chapter outlines the issues and suggests ways that campus leaders can help veterans who are women to adjust as they return to civilian life.

5. A Statewide Approach to Creating Veteran-Friendly 45
Campuses
Jayne M. Lokken, Donald S. Pfeffer, James McAuley, Christopher Strong
Meeting the needs of veterans has become a statewide priority in some places. This chapter explores how an institution of higher education collaborated with state agencies to offer enhanced services to veterans.

6. Ensuring the Success of Deploying Students: A Campus   55
View
Teresa Johnson
Developing programs to support student veterans is a campuswide task
that involves both faculty and personnel from various administrative
offices. This chapter details how, through the efforts of staff members,
Appalachian State University gained a reputation for being a veteran-
friendly campus.

7. Connections, Partnerships, Opportunities, and Programs to   61
Enhance Success for Military Students
Deborah Ford, Pamela Northrup, Lusharon Wiley
Colleges are better able to meet the needs of students when partnerships are formed with other committed service providers. At the University of West Florida, outreach efforts have resulted in programs to
address the learning needs of active military personnel.

8. Student Veterans Organizations   71
John Summerlot, Sean-Michael Green, Daniel Parker
Military service forms bonds among those who have experienced that
unique culture. This chapter examines the processes used to develop
student veterans organizations on campuses and the role of those organizations in providing support and connection for those who have had
the shared experience of military service.

9. Partnering to Assist Disabled Veterans in Transition   81
David DiRamio, Michele Spires
One of the ways that society is beginning to respond to the needs of
seriously wounded veterans is by connecting them with educational
opportunities. An innovative program designed to help wounded veterans access educational opportunities is sponsored by the American
Council on Education.

10. Stewards of the Public Trust: Federal Laws That Serve   89
Servicemembers and Student Veterans
Michael McGrevey, Darryl Kehrer
To effectively serve the needs of student veterans, campus administrators should be aware of the range of government-supported benefit programs that are available. This chapter provides a description of the
benefits and explains how to obtain additional information.

INDEX   95

EDITORS' NOTES

Throughout the rich history of this series and consistent with the goals of the student affairs profession, focus has been placed on meeting the needs of special student populations. This volume continues that tradition.

In the 1960s and 1970s, many veterans of the U.S. armed forces, on returning home from Vietnam, discovered that their service was not honored. The war effort had lost popular support, anti-war protests were common, and the country was divided. As a nation, we were unable or unwilling to separate an unpopular war from those who had been sent to fight it. College campuses, often the places where the protests were held, did not respond well to the needs of veterans who became students. And while it is likely that there were individuals who provided exceptional services, little in the literature from that era suggests that campus leaders in general and student affairs professionals in particular understood the needs of students who were making a transition from combat to campus.

During the early years of the twenty-first century, the United States is again a nation at war and, again, those who were sent to fight the wars are coming back and enrolling as students. While popular support for these wars is also an issue, society, including campuses, is responding in mostly positive ways to veterans of the wars in Iraq and Afghanistan. The contributors to this volume are persons who recognize the need to separate attitudes toward war from attitudes toward those who were sent to fight wars. The contributors are involved either as members of the higher education community or with issues related to higher education. The contributors have worked to understand the needs of students who are making the transition from military service, have participated in the development of programs in response to those needs, or have themselves experienced the transition from the military to the campus.

The purpose with which we approached this project was to share information and programmatic initiatives as a way of encouraging campus leaders to seriously and creatively become involved with students on their campuses who are also veterans. Such efforts would include identifying the needs of students and providing resources so that they can successfully achieve their academic goals.

Chapters One through Four are intended as a framework for understanding the experiences of those who have served in the military and then make the transition to college. Chapter One, which we coauthored with Regina L. Garza Mitchell, offers basic research about the current generation of students who have experienced war, using interviews with veterans from

NEW DIRECTIONS FOR STUDENT SERVICES, no. 126, Summer 2009   © Wiley Periodicals, Inc.
Published online in Wiley InterScience (www.interscience.wiley.com) • DOI: 10.1002/ss.310

the conflicts in Iraq and Afghanistan. The findings provide a starting point for understanding the contemporary issues facing students who are making the transition from combat to campus. Chapter Two, by Mark Bauman, extends the basic research theme by describing a study of students who served in National Guard and reserve units that were deployed to war zones. It focuses on how disruptive a call to duty can be for students who are still in school and how student services administrators and others on campus can support their deployment and return to college. In Chapter Three, Corey B. Rumann and Florence A. Hamrick provide a historical perspective on the relationship between higher education and students who have served in the military. They also offer suggestions for services and support programs that student affairs professionals can use to assist student veterans. Margaret Baechtold and Danielle M. De Sawal break new ground in Chapter Four with a piece about women veterans. Focusing on gender identity, they present information about the concerns of female students who have served in the military.

Chapters Five through Eight focus on programs that can help campuses become veteran-friendly by providing exemplars of good practices. Several of these initiatives are designed to extend services to the families of veterans. In the student services profession, we have always valued the sharing of ideas, and that is the intent of this group of chapters. Concern for the well-being of veterans is exhibited across society in various ways. In Chapter Five, Jayne M. Lokken, Donald S. Pfeffer, James McAuley, and Christopher Strong detail efforts to support military-affiliated students in Minnesota. They demonstrate how state agencies—including a college and university system office, an individual university within the system, and the veterans affairs department—collaborated to assist students and improve the chances for their success. In Chapter Six, Teresa Johnson shares lessons learned from her university, which has had a tradition of assisting veterans since the first Gulf War. In Chapter Seven, Deborah Ford, Pamela Northrup, and Lusharon Wiley offer ideas from their institution for creating partnerships and initiatives for veterans and active-duty military personnel who are students. Both Chapters Six and Seven provide important examples of programs and services for campus administrators to consider. Chapter Eight, by John Summerlot, Sean-Michael Green, and Daniel Parker, describes student veterans organizations, including their history, formation, and roles.

In an effort to provide specialized information, Chapter Nine, which David coauthored with Michele Spires, offers a look at a nationwide program that assists severely injured veterans in making a successful transition to college. Finally, in Chapter Ten, Michael McGrevey and Darryl Kehrer describe federal programs that are open to students who have served in the military, including information about GI Bill benefits that have become available since the September 11 attacks.

As you read this volume, keep in mind that the student services profession has a tradition of developing research-based programs to support the academic success of student populations with special needs. On some campuses, efforts are under way to identify and establish programs that recognize veterans as a student population with unique needs. In the course of working on this project, we spoke of the need to do research, to share information, and to advocate on behalf of student veterans. As you consider the issues raised in this book, think also of how you can provide that leadership on your campus in order to serve your students.

Robert Ackerman
David DiRamio
Editors

ROBERT ACKERMAN *is associate professor of higher education leadership at the University of Nevada, Las Vegas (UNLV), where he served as vice president for student services from 1986 to 2000. He edited* The Mid-Level Manager in Student Affairs *and was co-editor of* Student Freedom Revisited, *both publications of NASPA—Student Affairs Administrators in Higher Education. He is a founder of and faculty advisor to the UNLV Student Veterans Organization.*

DAVID DIRAMIO *is assistant professor of higher education administration at Auburn University. He has coauthored five research articles, including "From Combat to Campus: Voices of Student-Veterans" in the* NASPA *Journal. He serves as NASPA's liaison for an American Council on Education initiative to help severely injured veterans attend college.*

1

Twenty-five students who served in the Iraq or Afghanistan wars were interviewed. The findings suggest that combat veterans are a student population with special needs and require support from both policymakers and program providers.

Transitions: Combat Veterans as College Students

Robert Ackerman, David DiRamio,
Regina L. Garza Mitchell

The experience of war makes those who fight a special group within the general population. The purpose of our study was to investigate how combat veterans who become college students make the transition to campus life, in order to identify how administrators can acknowledge and support them. A total of six women and nineteen men were interviewed; twenty-four were enrolled full-time at one of three public research universities and one at a four-year regional university (DiRamio, Ackerman, and Mitchell, 2008). Of those interviewed, only two had experienced more than a single deployment to Iraq or Afghanistan. Nine participants had attended college prior to serving on active duty. Students still on active duty were not included in the study, although National Guard and reserve force members were. The authors conducted the interviews, and the decision to end the study at twenty-five cases was guided by researcher agreement that clear themes had emerged (Creswell, 1997).

Emergent Themes

Interviews with participants revealed similar experiences, and themes emerged relating to joining the military, deployment, serving in a war zone, and moving from combat into the classroom.

New Directions for Student Services, no. 126, Summer 2009   © Wiley Periodicals, Inc.
Published online in Wiley InterScience (www.interscience.wiley.com) • DOI: 10.1002/ss.311

5

Joining the Military

One morning when I woke up to go to school in my senior year of high school, I saw the 9/11 footage. Saw the airplanes go through, and that was when I decided, well, I'm gonna go enlist. [Marine reservist]

Motivation to join the service was the result of a combination of factors expressed as "wanting to do my duty," which included a desire to respond to the September 11 attacks, a sense of patriotism, and a desire to defend or protect the country. Several participants came from military families; one represented the fourth generation in his family to have served, the third to have been in combat. Three made the decision to enter the military while still in grade school. Along with patriotism, the promise of educational benefits was a primary motivator. Eight participants noted the need for financial support to attend college; one wanted the benefits so that she could provide a better life for her daughter. Five noted that the military offers adventure as an enticement and expressed that they wanted something challenging or that the service provided an escape or a change.

Deployment

I had to withdraw from college and, actually, I was doing great at the time. My thing was to try to finish school; I wasn't trying not to go overseas. It was just very upsetting to just have to withdraw in the middle of the semester like that, but I had to. [Army reservist]

Activations can occur during the academic year. One soldier received notice of deployment alert in March, but his activation orders were not received until mid-fall. He lost four semesters because he could not attend while on alert and then served thirteen months in Iraq. A member of the National Guard was deployed to New Orleans following Hurricane Katrina and then to Iraq; both deployments interrupted his education. A National Guard combat medic was activated twice; the first time was for seven months, and the second time included a year in Afghanistan. She had to reapply to a nursing program both times when she returned to college. The military units of two students were sent on back-to-back deployments, meaning that they each missed approximately six semesters.

   None of those who had to withdraw indicated difficulty in accomplishing that process, although some noted the difficulty of dealing with college-related administrative tasks while also preparing to deploy, making out a will, and managing the pressure of the situation. There are other consequences of withdrawing from college, not the least of which is financial. A soldier who was deployed withdrew from school and lost a scholarship because he was unable to complete the semester. Others were activated late in the semester and lost the work completed for those terms plus the monies

NEW DIRECTIONS FOR STUDENT SERVICES • DOI: 10.1002/ss

they had paid to attend. Before withdrawing, most talked with their instructors; one was able to reach an informal agreement with her instructors that she would complete the courses upon her return, which she did. None reported difficulty in dealing with professors in regard to these issues; all reported that their instructors were accommodating to the extent that they could be.

Serving in a War Zone

You are going to come back changed. It's not necessarily good or bad, but you will fundamentally be a different person. [National Guard]

Our intent was not to study in-country experiences; however, we learned of a relationship between those experiences and the transition to college. The experiences of combat do influence other aspects of life, including going to college. The observation reflected in the following comment was something we heard from many others:

"I think it [combat] helped me out a lot and it has given me a lot of self-discipline, establishing goals, time management, and everything. There are so many things you can get from the military to help you out as a college student." [Regular Army serviceperson]

A member of the National Guard described how being in combat changed her: "I took a lot from it. I made it a learning experience." For one serviceperson, the lesson was that people in the military do "serious things and that doing serious things becomes good preparation for being a serious college student." An Air Force veteran described the experience of arriving in Iraq along with all different kinds of people: "You grow up in a heartbeat. You really learn a lot about yourself." An Army officer who had served three deployments in Iraq and who was medically retired, however, noted that the killing and survival skills learned in the military were not applicable in classroom settings, implying that a relearning of leadership skills was also necessary.

There were constant reminders of the horrors of war. Losing friends who had been killed or injured and evacuated was particularly difficult. A student who had served in an Air Force support unit spoke of the death of a friend he had made who was in the Army as being "very hard for me, because we would meet, . . . have lunch together, and talk. Sometimes, because of work we could not connect. . . . He stopped coming to lunch, and I went to his commander and they told me."

Some had been wounded. A Marine veteran had had nine surgeries and was retired at 30 percent disability. He spoke of leaving behind "a very close-knit group of guys who I was protecting, watching their butts, [and] they were watching mine. I was forced to leave that involuntarily, and a lot of that had to do with leaving a brotherhood." A member of the National Guard

NEW DIRECTIONS FOR STUDENT SERVICES • DOI: 10.1002/ss

whose trucks had been blown up while he was driving lost hearing in one ear as a result. We spoke with a female National Guard member, also a truck driver, who had experienced two trucks blowing up but had escaped without physical injury.

A regular Army enlisted man spoke of his arrival in Iraq. He had just gotten there when a car bomb exploded a mile from the base. He recalled diving to the floor at the sound of the blast. The soldier next to him asked whether it was a mortar; he said, "I don't know; this is my first day." One of the authors wished an Army National Guard veteran a good day as the interview ended. She responded, "Any day you are not being shot at is a good day."

Being in a combat area is stressful; every veteran we interviewed had participated in, witnessed, or heard of horrific events. The women we interviewed had faced the additional factor of being in situations where they were not always welcomed by their fellow soldiers. One woman, a construction engineer in the National Guard, referred to her experience as being in a "double boys club" in which it was difficult to earn acceptance as a female soldier and as a female assigned to construction. A female Air Force tech sergeant and veteran of Bosnia and Iraq spoke of the difficulties of being among only a handful of women stationed on a base with thousands of men and having to learn to navigate complex social and work situations.

Although they had experienced war, none of the participants expressed regret at having been in combat; they were proud of their service, and some, but not all, said they would be willing to return. Some re-enlisted, and among their reasons for doing so was a desire to continue receiving educational benefits so that they could complete a degree program.

From Combat to the Classroom

It would be a great help not to be just thrown into college. All the paperwork and whatnot I have to go through, they could offer a little more help as far as that and other veteran's programs. I'm probably eligible for things I'm not aware of. And I have nobody here to go and talk to [to] find out about [them]. I'd like to see them actually have a Veteran's Department here. Because when I walked in, they just tossed a piece of paper at me and said, "Oh, here, fill this out." That does not help. [Regular Army serviceperson]

The focus of our study was the transition that combat veterans make when they become college students. For many with whom we spoke, this was the most difficult transition of all. Problems, when they arose, came from several sources. The Veterans Administration, which handles educational and medical benefits, is not an easy bureaucracy to understand, although some negotiated it well. We learned, too, that not all campuses have functioning programs in place to assist veterans who have become students. Then there were the challenges of fitting in, of just being a student.

At the end of deployments, the military provides debriefing opportunities as part of the activities of processing out of the combat zone. It was apparent from our interviews that these sessions vary in quality and effectiveness. A National Guard member spoke of "tons" of debriefing sessions in Iraq, Kuwait, and then stateside. He noted that for most, "80 percent did not apply. . . . You get in the habit of tuning it out since there is so much that does not apply." A member of the National Guard who had been debriefed after he returned to the United States said that the sessions consisted mainly of "how are you doing" questions. A guardsman suggested that he could have gotten better treatment, but to do so would have risked a delay in going home: "They kind of implied to us that if you have problems, you're going to stay longer; nobody wanted to stay longer."

Study participants noted several areas that were of concern during their transition to college:

Veterans Administration. The upcoming role of the Veterans Administration (VA) in the post-deployment lives of soldiers was outlined during their debriefings, sessions that apparently did not hold the attention of those who had just left combat zones and who very much wanted to get home. Many of those with whom we spoke described problems with the VA, problems that have received national attention. Some of those problems concerned the payment of educational benefits. An Air Force veteran complained, "It took eight or more weeks to receive benefits." In the meantime, he had to come up with out-of-pocket funds for tuition and related college costs. His complaint was echoed by others.

Members of the National Guard likely fared better than other servicepersons because each National Guard unit has an educational officer who can help sort out benefit issues. One example of this disparity involves transcripts of military training from the Army/American Council on Education Registry Transcript System. We spoke with several veterans who did not know that such a record existed, how a copy of the transcript could be obtained, or whether their college offered credit for military training. Generally, National Guard members had this information.

Campus veterans services offices and other campus support services. Campuses usually have a designated person to administer benefit programs for veterans. Several of the veterans in our interviews expressed appreciation for the support provided by veterans services personnel on their campus. On one of the campuses represented in our study, students had established close working relationships with staff in the veterans services office, who provided connections for students beyond the processing of educational benefits. In one of the other two situations, the program director was newly appointed and received mixed reviews. On the third campus, the veterans services office received only criticisms; veterans from that campus were unaware of any services available to them through the office.

We heard about an exceptional level of service provided by a veterans services office from a veteran who had transferred from another campus to one that was included in our survey. When his unit was deployed, staff from the veterans services office handled the withdrawals from classes, dealt with financial aid issues, and kept in contact with the soldiers while they were deployed by e-mailing campus news updates. When the deployment was over, the office staff initiated re-entry and benefits paperwork and assisted with registration for classes.

The students we spoke with mentioned "veteran-friendly campuses," and while that term was difficult to define, we came to understand that veterans used it to refer to campuses where programs and people were in place to assist with the transitions between college and the military (see Chapters Five, Six, and Eight). These campuses, like the one noted earlier, have made an active commitment to the success of veterans as students. An example of a campus that was not veteran-friendly illustrates the other extreme. A member of a National Guard unit, while in Iraq, made phone contact with the financial aid office at his home campus. He had withdrawn from classes when he was deployed, leaving behind a financial aid problem. He called the office, only to be told that to resolve the issue he had to come to the office, something that was not possible. He hung up in frustration, unable to convince the staff member in the financial aid office that there had to be a second option. By way of contrast, an Army reservist who had had two tours in Iraq said that the veterans services provider on his campus anticipated issues and offered suggestions and solutions even before the soldier realized there was a concern.

Re-entering civilian life and becoming a student. Even for those who had attended college prior to being deployed, there was an adjustment upon their return. A major aspect of the adjustment was relearning study skills. An Army reservist described it this way: "It's kind of like I forgot how I studied. Prior to leaving, I had a 3.4 GPA, and when I got back, it just went down." After having been away from school and formal classroom instruction, re-entry was difficult. Several students mentioned the need for an orientation to college programs just for veterans.

While some adjustment issues could be attributed to being away from school for an extended period of time, post-traumatic stress disorder (PTSD) was also a factor. A member of the Army Reserves commented, "I think I was a better student when I came back . . . but what made it hard was my attention span and my patience were very short, so sitting in class . . . became very hard to do." A member of the regular Army said this about adjusting: "Once I got back to school, it was like I know what I need to do and it is right in front of me, but I'm just not doing it. I don't know if it [is] because I am not as focused as I was before I left, or . . . I don't know."

This same person mentioned that when he returned from a year of driving supply trucks between Kuwait and Iraq, he could not sleep at night. Several of the veterans talked about anger and stress as a carryover from their time in combat. The memories of war, of being on constant alert, and of being afraid remained close to the surface and were, for some, difficult to manage. An Army veteran said that he disliked being in large groups of people, that he was no longer a very social person, and that he always looked mean. An Army reservist who had spent thirteen months in combat talked about having to keep busy because if he was not busy, he would become depressed. He had not had those symptoms prior to being deployed. A sergeant in the National Guard reported that after more than a year in Iraq, "even my girlfriend noticed the changes. . . . Pretty much everyone that I went over with, I mean, we've all got anger issues now, like it kind of falls down as time goes on, but, man, it just doesn't take much to get sparked off and go . . ."

An Army officer who spent a year in Iraq talked about the adjustment after coming home: "It is really hard adjusting, coming back from a war zone into the United States. . . . It seemed like for a whole month, I did just a whole bunch of jigsaw puzzles just to clear my mind and keep myself, I don't know, just to settle myself down and kinda adjust back to life. I've got hundreds of puzzles that I did during just that one month, so I guess that was just my way of coping." Several of those with whom we spoke mentioned having to develop similar coping strategies after leaving combat. A soldier who drove supply trucks in Iraq said she sold her SUV when she got home because she was afraid she would drive it like it was a truck and she was back in Iraq. Another veteran of two tours in Iraq mentioned that he could no longer sit for extended periods of time and that he had to explain his need to get up and walk around the classroom to his professors.

With only a few exceptions, the veterans in our study did not report conflicts with others over the fact that they had served. Still, unfortunate incidents happened. In one, a sociology professor "referred to the American soldier as a terrorist" in a class in which a combat veteran was a student. In protest, the veteran did not complete the final exam and failed the course. In another incident, a Marine who served in Afghanistan was called a traitor in class by another student because he expressed opposition to the war. Generally, the veterans in our sample did not bring attention to their service and discussed it in class only when they deemed it appropriate. Some have been thanked for their service; some have been asked questions about what it was like to be in combat; and at least three reported that they had been asked whether they had killed anyone, a question each found disturbing and difficult to respond to. Several remained in the reserves and wore their uniforms on campus as they came and went from military-related activities. None reported negative incidents associated with wearing the uniform.

Not surprisingly, participants offered suggestions about what campuses could do to assist veterans in their transition to college. Almost every participant spoke about efforts to identify veterans on campus and about being dependent for support on others who have had similar experiences. A Marine who had served in Iraq explained, "People who I would consider my best friends here still can not relate to me on certain levels as far as the experiences I've had. You just can't relate unless you have been there. Those people have. Those relationships are still very strong and very important."

NEW DIRECTIONS FOR STUDENT SERVICES • DOI: 10.1002/ss

Many students in our study expressed concerns about friends who were still deployed and about how the sacrifices required by a nation at war do not fall equally on all persons.

Study participants described the structured life of the military and how difficult it was to move from a strictly defined structure to a loosely configured campus where there was no chain of command from which to get answers. A four-year Air Force veteran said that going from "something that is so structured and so routine, and on task . . . then just to be released and you have to make your own schedule, some people find that hard." His suggestion, which we also heard from others, was that campuses offer orientation sessions for veterans by veterans.

Discussion and Conclusions

My campus has vastly improved their services for soldiers and veterans since the time I first started attending college in 2001. They lay it out for you and show you the different steps that need to be taken to get the benefits that we have been promised. One thing that has been a struggle is that you have to be proactive. [National Guard]

As of March 2007, just over 1.5 million members of the armed services had been deployed and had served in either Iraq or Afghanistan (Defense Manpower Data Center, 2007). As these conflicts continue, the number of combat veterans who become college students will likely increase. Given what we have learned about assisting the members of special needs student populations to achieve their educational goals, it would be a disservice to treat veterans as if they were invisible.

Veterans represent a potential campus resource. They have had leadership experiences and confronted difficult challenges, challenges that have matured and, perhaps, hardened them. Many joined the military to earn educational benefits so that they could realize the opportunities available through higher education. Our work was an effort to learn about the transitions that combat veterans make when they enroll as students. What we learned from the participants in this study suggests that combat veterans who become students represent a population with special needs and that there are ways for campus personnel to work with these students to effectively meet those needs. The following principles provide some guidelines.

- Deployments represent disruptive, life-altering transitions (Schlossberg, Waters, and Goodman, 1995). Colleges should develop student-centered activation and deployment policies that manage the campus bureaucracy so as not to further complicate what is already a stressful situation for those called to active military duty.
- Students who are deployed benefit when their campus maintains a connection with them.

- Veterans who enroll as students experience difficulties. Thought needs to be given to the responsibilities assigned by the campus to the veterans services officer. Campuses meet the needs of other special student populations through offices whose mission is to provide specifically designed support services. In planning those services, efforts should be made to know the students who constitute the veteran population (Kuh, Kinzie, Schuh, and Whitt, 2005).
- Campuses are encouraged to meet the challenge of becoming veteran-friendly by putting in place personnel, policies, resources, and programs that reflect sensitivity to and understanding of the needs of veterans. Supporting the troops should be an action plan, not just a happy slogan.
- There is an urgent need to share best practices, to exchange ideas, and to conduct research that will provide campuses with the information needed to promote the academic achievement of veterans who are students.

In addition, it is important to note that although gender issues were not part of our study, we heard from female veterans that they faced unique and difficult challenges because of their gender and the male-dominated traditions of the military. Evidence supports the reality of these concerns (Corbett, 2007; Cohen, 2006). These issues are so significant, in part because of the likelihood of negative post-trauma psychological effects on victims, that sexual trauma has become a recognized problem in the treatment of veterans (Street and Stafford, 2007). Campuses must be prepared to provide support to those who have had to deal with sexual harassment and assault by other military personnel while confronting the dangers of combat (see Chapter Four).

Similarly, while mental health issues were not a focus of our study, several of the veterans we interviewed indicated that they were attempting to cope with depression, with PTSD, and with other mental health issues stemming from their service. Approximately 20 percent of service personnel returning from Iraq report mental health problems (Hoge, Auchterlonie, and Milliken, 2006); some studies put the figure of returning veterans who have received mental health or psychosocial diagnoses at over 30 percent (Seal and others, 2007), and data cited by the Department of Defense Task Force on Mental Health (2007) suggest that 27 percent of returning veterans report significant depression, 24 percent report alcohol abuse issues, and 43 percent report problems with anger. Research suggests that deployments of longer than six months and multiple deployments contribute to an increase in mental health issues (Department of Defense Mental Health Advisory Team, 2007). Campuses need to be prepared to meet the needs of veterans who would benefit from mental health support services. In addition, four of the veterans we interviewed had combat-related physical injuries that required accommodations under the Americans with Disabilities Act and Section 504 of the Rehabilitation Act of 1973 (see Chapter Nine).

It is likely that as the Iraq and Afghanistan conflicts continue, so will the demand for specialized support services for veterans on campus.

References

Cohen, S. "Equal Opportunity War." *Las Vegas Review Journal,* Dec. 10, 2006, pp. 1J–3J.

Corbett, S. "The Women's War." *New York Times,* Mar. 18, 2007, p. 42.

Creswell, J. W. *Qualitative Inquiry and Research Design.* Thousand Oaks, Calif.: Sage, 1997.

Defense Manpower Data Center. *CTS Deployment File Baseline Report (March 31).* Washington, D.C.: U.S. Department of Defense, 2007.

Department of Defense Mental Health Advisory Team. "Survey Results, 2007." [http://defenselink.mil/release.aspx?releaseid=10824]. 2007. Retrieved May 4, 2007.

Department of Defense Task Force on Mental Health. *An Achievable Vision: Report of the Department of Defense Task Force on Mental Health.* Falls Church, Va.: Defense Health Board, 2007.

DiRamio, D., Ackerman, R., and Mitchell, R. "From Combat to Campus: Voices of Student-Veterans." *NASPA Journal,* 2008, *45*(1), 73–102.

Hoge, C. W., Auchterlonie, J. L., and Milliken, C. S. "Mental Health Problems, Use of Mental Health Services, and Attrition from Military Service After Returning from Deployment to Iraq or Afghanistan." *Journal of the American Medical Association,* 2006, *295*(9), 1023–1032.

Kuh, G. D., Kinzie, J., Schuh, J. H., and Whitt, E. J. *Student Success in College: Creating Conditions That Matter.* San Francisco: Jossey-Bass, 2005.

Schlossberg, N. K., Waters, E. B., and Goodman, J. *Counseling Adults in Transition.* (2nd. ed.) New York: Springer, 1995.

Seal, K. H., Bertenthal, D., Miner, C. R., Sen, S., and Marmar, C. "Bringing the War Home." *Archives of Internal Medicine,* 2007, *167*(5), 476–482.

Street, A., and Stafford, J. *Military Sexual Trauma: Caring for Veterans.* Washington, D.C.: Department of Veterans Affairs, National Center for PSTD, 2007.

ROBERT ACKERMAN *is associate professor of higher education leadership at the University of Nevada, Las Vegas. He served in the U.S. Navy.*

DAVID DIRAMIO *is assistant professor of higher education administration at Auburn University. He served in the U.S. Navy.*

REGINA L. GARZA MITCHELL *is assistant professor of educational leadership at Central Michigan University.*

NEW DIRECTIONS FOR STUDENT SERVICES • DOI: 10.1002/ss

2

This chapter provides insight into the separation and return processes experienced when undergraduate National Guard and reserve personnel are mobilized for military duty. Suggestions for faculty and administrative staff on how to assist these individuals throughout this process are provided.

The Mobilization and Return of Undergraduate Students Serving in the National Guard and Reserves

Mark Bauman

The current utilization of U.S. reserve troops is the largest since the Korean War (Griffith, 2005). As of April 1, 2008, reserve and National Guard service personnel numbered 7,800 in Afghanistan (O'Bryant and Waterhouse, 2008a). In Iraq, 27,900 of the military force consist of reserve or National Guard personnel (O'Bryant and Waterhouse, 2008b). The timing of the mobilization of National Guard and reserve personnel is often ". . . unpredictable and the duration of their active duty may not be known when they are deployed . . ." (Reeves, Parker, and Konkle-Parker, 2005, p. 932). This unpredictability results in uncertainty for the National Guard or reserve member and his or her family.

Some reserve and National Guard personnel are enrolled in college. Much like those who choose not to attend college, reservists and Guard members who are students are challenged by issues of separation from family and employment. However, members of the reserves and National Guard who are college students must also separate from their educational endeavors, often for two or more academic terms, without knowing the precise date of their return. Upon release from active duty, veterans attempting to make the transition back into academic culture face challenges; thus, it is appropriate that this unique subpopulation of students be better understood.

The purpose of this chapter is to examine the military mobilization process as it affects students. What is the process by which students who

NEW DIRECTIONS FOR STUDENT SERVICES, no. 126, Summer 2009   © Wiley Periodicals, Inc.
Published online in Wiley InterScience (www.interscience.wiley.com) • DOI: 10.1002/ss.312

are called to active military duty prepare for mobilization, separate from the institution, and then re-enroll upon their release from active duty? This study spans three phases of the military mobilization process. During the first phase, *pre-mobilization,* students "throttle up" in preparation for active-duty deployment. During the second phase, *separation,* students withdraw from their institution and are often disconnected from it for the length of their deployment. In the third phase, *return,* students "throttle down" from military service and resume their college education.

Dual Roles: Students and National Guard or Reserve Members

Disruptive deployments for military members are similar to the phenomenon of "stopping out" for the civilian college student. The term *stopping out* is used to refer to ". . . students who do not complete their plan of study within the normal time schedule, having skipped a term or more and then having returned to college" (Hoyt and Winn, 2004, p. 397). Students who stop out of college mimic the enrollment patterns of mobilized military members.

The component of the stopping-out process that is most relevant to this study is the re-enrollment experience. Numerous variables influence a student's experience as they return to college. Kasworm's meta-analysis of research on enrollment reveals that returning students often have difficulty entering a youthful culture (Kasworm, 1990). Thus, campus personnel who are indifferent to the issues of students who are returning from military service may also be unprepared to address the needs of returning adult learners. Steltenpohl and Shipton and (1986) suggest that returning adult students may feel marginalized or inadequate as they make the transition to the college setting. Research by Glass and Harshberger (1974) confirmed this phenomenon of disinterest during the Vietnam War era, asserting that faculty and staff would be ". . . ill-equipped to handle these new students, both in terms of attitude and theory base" (p. 212).

When students are called to military service, they must put their college plans on hold, and because a typical deployment lasts up to eighteen months, it may be two semesters or more before they are able to return to college. This deferment means that when they return, they will have the same academic standing as students often years younger. Just as Glass and Harshberger (1974) asked in regard to returning Vietnam veterans, we should also ask whether faculty, staff, and campus administrators are prepared and equipped to work with students who are called to or returning from military service.

During the separation phase of military service, students are generally disconnected from their institution, both physically and socially. A small effort on the part of an institution can help the student-soldier maintain connections to his or her campus (see Chapter Six).

Mental health problems represent some of the more formidable challenges faced by returning veterans, including activated reservists. Of course, the mental health of student combat veterans needs to be understood by those on campus who are charged with providing support services. Hoge, Auchterlonie, and Milliken (2006) reported that nearly 18 percent of Army soldiers and Marines returning from Iraq were diagnosed with post-traumatic stress disorder (PTSD), according to the military's own screening instruments. In a follow-up study, the same authors observed a substantial increase in the presence of PTSD, noting that 30–35 percent of all returning veterans screened positive for PTSD; incidence among reserve veterans was at the high end of the range at 35 percent (Milliken, Auchterlonie, and Hoge, 2007). Unfortunately, specific data on military personnel who return to college from service in combat zones, including information about those who have screened positive for mental health challenges, is unavailable at present. However, statistics for the general population of veterans suggest that mental health issues are a salient concern.

Interviews with Undergraduate National Guard and Reserve Members

Collecting personal accounts was chosen as the best method for an exploratory study of how the military mobilization process affects enlisted undergraduates. Twenty-four students at two institutions were interviewed. One student was a Marine reservist, one student was an Army reservist, and all others ($n = 22$) were members of the Army National Guard. Each of the twenty-four participants had been mobilized for military duty in the Middle East, requiring them to separate from college.

Phase One: Pre-Mobilization. The pre-mobilization phase encompasses time prior to mobilization. It is often filled with rumors and speculation, mostly confined to the unit but also within the larger political context. The common military phrase "hurry up and wait" aptly captures the essence of how the interviewees described the pre-mobilization phase. During this phase, students felt a mixture of nervousness and excitement. Luis, a twenty-seven-year-old former active-duty Army member who was an Army National Guardsman when he was deployed to Iraq, recalled, ". . . Being infantryman, being deployed to a combat zone, it's like getting to play in the Olympics. Everybody was really excited; almost everybody volunteered." John, a twenty-two-year-old veteran who had been in Iraq, provided further insight: ". . . I was kind of excited to go. Even though it's a war zone, it's a whole different experience. You don't know what to expect and that excitement that, like, I can't wait to go and do my part."

During the first phase, the chatter around a member's unit clearly suggests that deployment is imminent. However, without official military orders showing a precise exit date, many are reluctant to take definitive action on important matters pertaining to school, work, or family. Many said that multiple dates for activation came and went before anything official ever occurred. In many ways, this is the thinking phase. A member of the reserves or the National Guard may be thinking, "What should I do with my apartment? What will I do if I'm close to finishing the semester but have to leave? Whom should I tell?" Talking and planning with family members, preparing one's gear, attending drill, and getting more connected with one's military buddies are also important during this phase. Moreover, a sense of one's dual role is even stronger in the pre-mobilization phase. Tina, a former Marine reservist, provides a thoughtful account of the push and pull of role conflict: "It wasn't easy, going from a student to an NCO (non-commissioned officer) and from an NCO back to a student. As a student, you're supposed to question everything you're told. . . . You're supposed to always think outside the box, challenge rhetoric and plans made by authority. As a Marine, you are supposed to accept orders without question . . . no matter how little they make sense. The roles and rules of a student are very different than those of a Marine. . . . There's very little overlap."

Marcus, a twenty-six-year-old Army National Guard member finishing his second deployment, remarked in a similar fashion: ". . . Being a civilian soldier is a tough job. While the regular army just balances the Army life as its job, the National Guard and reserve components have a lot more to deal with. In most cases, the reserve soldiers are either in school or have a full-time job. When it comes time to be called up, a lot of people find it very difficult to adjust to this, especially those that have smaller children. I have now been deployed two times, and each time it gets a little harder, but it is still rewarding."

Phase Two: Separation. The separation phase is generally the longest of the three, beginning when receipt of orders marks a shift from rumor to reality. For many, the separation phase is when the emotional aspect of deployment begins. Daniel, a twenty-four-year-old former Army National Guardsman, recounts a moment shortly before he was to leave for training at Camp Shelby in Mississippi: "I remember we had a little ceremony before we left for Camp Shelby, Mississippi; we got back from the ceremony, and he [his father] couldn't get out of his car because he was crying and he didn't want to cry in front of me. That was the first time I ever saw him react. And that was probably the most disturbing thing for me or the saddest thing for me. I ended up crying as well with him."

Daniel's comment is quite similar to those of many from this sample; many—especially the men—remembered how their father reacted to their departure. Most reactions involved tears, something that these young men had rarely seen in their father. Interview data revealed that emotionally charged departures are also experienced with close friends, who must compete for time with the military member's family. By the time separation occurs, school-related tasks have been completed. In fact, data from the interviews showed that separation from one's educational institution, including faculty members and school friends, is often one of the first tasks to be completed once orders are finalized.

Separation also includes immersion into full active military service. Immersion includes the obvious physical tasks such as preparing gear, fulfilling various training requirements, and completing administrative duties. But there is also a shift toward socialization with fellow servicemembers that begins in this phase. Bob, a twenty-three-year-old Iraq veteran, recalled, "Being . . . deployed . . . really made me get closer with people in my unit. Before that, I wasn't social with them since they looked at me as a bad soldier (since I missed so many drills), so being there really made everyone a family. I've gotten closer with people, and I know I'm going be friends with them for a lifetime."

Adjusting from civilian life to active-duty military service challenged even the hardiest of individuals. Nearly all participants agreed that deployment was a stressful change of environment that required nearly constant alertness. However, during the interviews, most participants tried to focus more on the positive outcomes of their time "in country," a term used by military personnel to refer to time spent in a combat zone, instead of dwelling on disturbing and stressful experiences. Ryan, a twenty-two-year-old Iraq veteran, provided a seemingly matter-of-fact accounting that is unpleasant, yet reflective:

> I was stationed in the worst place; it's called Ramadi. I'm sure you've seen it on TV. It was terrible and it was good in the same way. I could tell you the bad parts all day. And the good parts, and you'll laugh. Granted, I lost eleven friends over there. We all wear bracelets for them. And that's terrible. But again, I made so many good friends. I've bettered myself in so many ways over there. It's unbelievable. It's war. You're going to lose people. That's the hardest part, you know? And then, ah . . . you build so much confidence. I've done things that a lot of people wouldn't do in this world.

During his interview, Ryan skimmed over the horror of losing eleven comrades and tried to emphasize the positive. In fact, interviews revealed that during the separation phase, everyone is exposed to an extremely stressful environment and, in turn, everyone finds his or her own way of coping with this stress. It might not make much sense to an outsider such as a student services professional, but it works for a person in uniform.

Most students from this sample made a clean break with their undergraduate institution during the separation phase. But it is during this phase that campus personnel can make a profound difference. Kathy, a twenty-four-year-old member of the National Guard and a veteran who served in Kuwait and Iraq, maintained a connection with one faculty member. Her "hero," as she recalled, helped her schedule her classes, rectify a financial matter, and reconnect with housing opportunities. And these efforts all occurred while Kathy was still "over there."

Another example of institutional "heroism" was reported by Carly, who maintained ties with her nursing faculty. Carly speaks highly of her nursing research class, which she completed while serving in Iraq:

> They let me take that [nursing research] while I was gone. The nursing department actually gave me an award while I was gone. And last year at their pinning,

NEW DIRECTIONS FOR STUDENT SERVICES • DOI: 10.1002/ss

apparently it was emotional and everyone was crying. I was still included in the pinning process of what was supposed to be my class. I communicated back and forth with them on e-mail; they sent me lots of packages. They were helpful with getting all my paperwork to my mom. And Dr. ____was really good, too; she communicated a lot with my parents. And it helped my parents a lot, too.

Based on insights from Carly and Kathy, it is clear that campus personnel should explore how to maintain ties with mobilized students. These connections should be more intentional than Kathy's experience, which was somewhat accidental. If she had not reached out to someone on campus, it is unclear whether the helpful communication would have occurred. Campus leaders should advocate policies and programs that encourage faculty or staff to maintain connections with military members throughout the three mobilization phases.

Phase Three: Return. The return phase begins as military personnel return to the United States. Participants reported having mixed feelings once they were home. Daniel's departure to Iraq had moved his father to tears, while it was Luis's return from Iraq that brought out his father's emotions. Luis, a twenty-seven-year-old former active-duty Army man turned Army National Guardsman, recalled the moment: ". . . I saw my dad cry. It broke my heart to see him cry, but it was the happiest I had ever been. It was an awesome feeling." For others, different emotions emerged. Only weeks before, these warriors had awakened each day with a clear purpose and a sense of duty and responsibility, and now they were effectively unemployed. Albert recalled pointedly that "the glory balloon pops." Returning servicemembers were considered heroes as they walked in their hometown parade, but after the initial rush of homecoming, some found themselves without direction and purpose. Alan collected unemployment for a time before he took a job doing manual labor. Carly expressed bitterness about her situation as she recounted filing for unemployment. But for Carly (and others in the study), the feelings ran deeper:

> I didn't want to have to face all that. I didn't want to face going back to school and nobody being here. I didn't want to face filing for unemployment because I no longer had a job. Or because I no longer had a purpose. It took me a while. Even a couple months ago, around spring break, I was feeling really down in the dumps because I feel completely worthless here. I was, like, what's the point of this? Will I ever get the gratification of helping people as a nurse as I did while I was gone [in Iraq]?

While returning home presents challenges, returning to school presents others. Veterans from this sample often found themselves lost when navigating the GI Bill benefits process, other tuition assistance programs, scheduling, or other administrative tasks associated with college attendance. Responses from veterans in this sample indicated how little the veterans ser-

NEW DIRECTIONS FOR STUDENT SERVICES • DOI: 10.1002/ss

vices office on campus was used. This obvious starting point for the academic return process appeared to be of little value. Instead, veterans in this study reported relying on informal mechanisms for navigating the return process, including calling or sending e-mails of inquiry to various offices on campus or finding an old friend who had remained in school to assist them. Data from the interviews point to the idea that formal return processes or orientations for returning veterans provided by the school would be of great benefit.

Robert, a twenty-seven-year-old veteran who served in two deployments, remarked, "The veterans office there [at his university] should have a more permanent presence than just the volunteer students and their spontaneous schedules. . . . It sucks that we have to play phone tag to handle something military-based instead of getting extra help because we put our lives on the line for them but they only give us three minutes of their time on the phone."

However, Robert also made a comment that described something similar to Kathy's idea of the campus "hero"—someone on campus who makes a difference: "Not all the experience was bad. There was this one lady who proved to be more than a great help to me and clearly went out of her way to assist in the grant procedures. . . ." Insights from Robert, Kathy, and Carly reinforce the notion that one individual at a university who connects with a veteran can make a meaningful and lasting impression on that student's experience.

One of the more difficult aspects of returning to college reported by the participants was the realization that everything has changed. Alan stated, ". . . You think that somebody pushed pause, you left for a while, and when you come back, they press play." Often, returning student veterans find that their original peer group has graduated, while their own class standing has remained unchanged and they are some years older than their new peers. But there is clearly more to the return experience than just a change in status or falling behind in credits.

Mental health challenges for returning service personnel were mentioned in the interviews. Ryan, the young man who "lost eleven friends over there," provided a pointed reflection: "We all have PTSD. It's bad. We've seen so much over there. And I got in trouble. I got a DUI. Soon as I started walking [after the DUI incident], I started hitting the gym again. I went to a bar—me and my buddies—eight of us, eight veterans together. Two of these guys talk off to us. We end up beating them up. It was bad; we hurt them. And I blacked out. So I had to see—I saw a counselor."

Unresolved emotions based on experiences in Iraq were a problem for some returning veterans in the study. Several participants cited difficulties in dealing with stress upon returning home. Most tied this difficulty to time served in a combat zone. John provided an example: "I was jumpy [when I returned home]; I was a total prick. And every little thing, when I heard the Fourth of July when I got back home, that was nuts. Because I thought it was either a mortar or gunshots. And when I'm driving, I'm always checking for IEDs or those roadside bombs, or when I go under a bridge, I slow down. I try to go for my weapon. I have a hard time sleeping."

Daniel reflected on the time period shortly after he arrived home: ". . . I don't know how much you want [referring to his disclosure], but I had a .45 [handgun] at home, and I ended up pulling it out and looking at it for a while and really debating suicide." Of the twenty-four participants, two reported contemplating suicide. Clearly, the mental health problems faced by some student veterans present unique challenges for higher education professionals.

Summary and Suggestions for Practice

I encourage college and university leaders to consider the findings of this study as a starting point for strategizing about ways to support veterans. It is important to understand the veteran experience from the unique perspective of students and begin a campus conversation about the issues raised. Such a conversation could take the form of open forums in which all members of the campus community are invited to discuss veterans' concerns, develop plans for institutional support, and dedicate appropriate resources to address the concerns. These efforts need to be intentional, not passive. Of course, examining best practices from other institutions would be helpful. Campus administrators should consider the idea of encouraging campus "heroes" who reach out to student veterans. Institutional leaders can assist by identifying individuals who demonstrate interest in helping and empower them to make a difference. Campus personnel can then form connections with student veterans, providing emotional support and guidance throughout the stages of mobilization, separation, and return.

Moreover, higher education professionals should take on the responsibility of easing the administrative burdens faced by students who are veterans. When possible, administrators and faculty could simplify the mobilization, departure, and return process. Regardless of which approach to assistance and support is taken, the important point is to start the conversation. Without the beginnings of a dialogue, the success of our student veterans will continue to be threatened.

References

Glass, J. C., and Harshberger, R. F. "The Full-Time, Middle-Aged Adult Student in Higher Education." *Journal of Higher Education*, 1974, *45*, 211–218.
Griffith, J. "Will Citizens Be Soldiers? Examining Retention of Reserve Component Soldiers." *Armed Forces & Society*, 2005, *31*, 353–383.
Hoge, C. W., Auchterlonie, J. L., and Milliken, C. S. "Mental Health Problems, Use of Mental Health Services, and Attrition from Military Service After Returning from Deployment to Iraq or Afghanistan." *Journal of the American Medical Association*, 2006, *295*(9), 1023–1032.
Hoyt, J. E., and Winn, B. A. "Understanding Retention and College Student Bodies: Differences Between Drop-Outs, Stop-Outs, Opt-Outs and Transfer-Outs." *NASPA Journal*, 2004, *41*, 395–417.

Kasworm, C. E. "Adult Undergraduates in Higher Education: A Review of Past Research Perspectives." *Review of Educational Research*, 1990, *60*, 345–372.

Milliken, C. S., Auchterlonie, J. L., and Hoge, C. W. "Longitudinal Assessment of Mental Health Problems Among Active and Reserve Component Soldiers Returning from the Iraq War." *Journal of the American Medical Association*, 2007, *298*(18), 2141–2148.

O'Bryant, J., and Waterhouse, M. "CRS Report for Congress: U.S. Forces in Afghanistan." [http://www.fas.org/sgp/crs/natsec/RS22633.pdf]. 2008a. Retrieved July 12, 2008.

O'Bryant, J., and Waterhouse, M. "CRS Report for Congress: U.S. Forces in Iraq." [http://ftp.fas.org/sgp/crs/mideast/RS22449.pdf]. 2008b. Retrieved July 12, 2008.

Reeves, R. R., Parker, J. D., and Konkle-Parker, D. J. "War-Related Mental Health Problems of Today's Veterans." *Psychiatric Annals*, 2005, *35*(11), 930–942.

Steltenpohl, E., and Shipton, J. "Facilitating a Successful Transition to College for Adults." *Journal of Higher Education*, 1986, *57*(6), 637–658.

MARK BAUMAN is a member of the student life staff at Bloomsburg University. This chapter is based on his dissertation research at Pennsylvania State University, where he is a doctoral candidate. He is also a reservist with the U.S. Coast Guard.

NEW DIRECTIONS FOR STUDENT SERVICES • DOI: 10.1002/ss

3

This chapter outlines major trends in supporting student veterans at colleges and universities, including ways that campus professionals can initiate programs and services to assist this emerging population of students.

Supporting Student Veterans in Transition

Corey B. Rumann, Florence A. Hamrick

The purpose of this chapter is to offer frameworks and considerations for student affairs professionals seeking to serve the transition needs of the current generation of student veterans. The historical intersections of the military and higher education, particularly with respect to the effects of the draft on students and higher education, training students for wartime purposes, and providing educational benefits to student veterans, are discussed. As the United States continues to rely on National Guard and reserve forces, enrolled students' concurrent military service has become a more common experience, and postsecondary educational benefits present an attractive incentive for military enlistment. At the same time, contemporary administrators and faculty members are less likely than earlier generations to have personally experienced military or wartime service. Consequently, campus personnel should initiate partnerships with veterans organizations and local military representatives in order to design and offer transitional services. Moreover, offering educational programs can build awareness of soldiers' experiences and assist campus administrators in being proactive in serving student veterans.

Preparing Soldiers and Educating Veterans

Dating from colonial times, long-standing suspicions of a powerful, professional standing military (Neiberg, 2000; Smith, 1985) fostered early development of local citizen-soldier militias (Neiberg, 2000), and college

NEW DIRECTIONS FOR STUDENT SERVICES, no. 126, Summer 2009 © Wiley Periodicals, Inc.
Published online in Wiley InterScience (www.interscience.wiley.com) • DOI: 10.1002/ss.313

campuses became primary sites of access to and development of citizen-soldiers for military service (Neiberg, 2000; Gruber, 1975). This relationship between higher education and the military was strengthened with the passage of the 1862 Morrill Act, which established military training programs at land-grant institutions (Abrams, 1989; Neiberg, 2000). One year prior to the United States' entrance into World War I, Congress passed the 1916 National Defense Act (NDA), and colleges and universities assumed a leading role in training soldiers via the ultimately short-lived Students' Army Training Corps (Gruber, 1975). In addition, the NDA created the "three components of the American military system still in use today: the active-duty forces, the organized reserves, and the National Guard" (Neiberg, 2000, p. 23). NDA legislation also created the Reserve Officers' Training Corps (ROTC) that standardized the heretofore independently organized training programs at colleges and universities (Gruber, 1975; Neiberg, 2000).

Created in part to forestall economic and societal problems related to discharging large numbers of World War II soldiers, the Servicemen's Readjustment Act of 1944 (popularly known as the GI Bill) granted educational and other economic benefits to returning veterans. Veterans entered higher education in unprecedented numbers, nearly overwhelming the system (Olson, 1974) and changing the face of postsecondary education. Numerous policy and programmatic changes were implemented by colleges and universities that enrolled World War II veterans. For the most part, this influx of students was managed satisfactorily through increasing class sizes, offering accelerated program completion schedules, allowing more flexible admission practices, hiring additional faculty members, offering academic credit for military experience, and accommodating family housing needs (Olson, 1974). In return, veterans proved to be responsible, mature, successful, and highly focused on their academic program (Olson, 1974; Toven, 1945).

The Korean War and Vietnam War eras introduced somewhat different sets of circumstances for veterans. For example, GI Bill benefits were available to Korean War veterans but smaller numbers enrolled in college upon discharge compared with World War II veterans (Olson, 1974). Although anti-war activism and anti-military activism did not originate with the Vietnam War, they were more widespread on college campuses during this time (Horan, 1990). In part because of changing public sentiment, veterans reported feeling unwelcome on campuses and attempted to maintain a low profile as students (Horan, 1990).

Evolutions of GI Bill provisions are discussed in detail in other chapters of this volume. Over time, educational benefit programs for veterans have incorporated multiple factors such as length of service and full-time or part-time military status to determine the total educational benefits that may be expended before, during, or after service. The 1985 Montgomery GI Bill extended educational benefits to National Guard and reserve members (Asch, Fair, and Kilburn, 2000). Federal legislation to provide veterans with educational benefits continues to be debated, so additional changes are likely in the future. In fact, the Post 9/11 GI Bill, which goes into effect on August 1, 2009, will increase educational benefits for many veterans who have served since September 11, 2001 (Military.com, 2008).

The All-Volunteer Force and Educational Incentives

From the time it was established in 1917, conscription into active military duty via the Selective Service System (SSS) was the principal means of ensuring that the personnel needs and operational requirements of the armed forces were met, particularly during wartime. During the Korean War, conscription deferments began to be granted for college attendance. While student deferments were not automatic and did not guarantee exemption from service, college enrollment became a draft avoidance strategy for some. Although SSS registration is still required of adult men, the active draft ended in 1973 and the U.S. military became an all-volunteer force. Developing appropriate recruitment incentives became a paramount consideration, particularly during times when recruitment fell short of established goals (Asch, Kilburn, and Klerman, 1999; Asch and Loughran, 2004).

The transition to the all-volunteer force also increased reliance on National Guard and reserve units for active-duty service, making their roles in military operations more prominent and, at times, essential. While National Guard and reserve troops had frequently been activated during the Korean War, these units were used on a more limited basis during the Vietnam War (Doubler and Listman, 2007).

Both the National Guard and the reserves play important roles in supplementing full-time active-duty military forces, although they differ operationally and structurally. Reserve troops operate under federal jurisdiction (that is, the president as commander-in-chief) and frequently are mobilized to respond to events that threaten national security and when the U.S. military is engaged in military operations during wartime (United States Army Reserve, 2008).

As descendants of state militias, National Guard units operate under the jurisdiction and command of the governors of their respective states. National Guard troops tend to be activated to address domestic emergencies that are not military in nature. For example, National Guard troops from across the country led rescue and relief efforts in the aftermath of Hurricane Katrina (Doubler and Listman, 2007). However, under a new framework for national security, the president can activate National Guard troops to serve overseas in war.

During peacetime, members of both forces are required to serve one weekend a month and two weeks a year for drill and training (Army National Guard, 2008). During times of war, both forces become available for deployment into combat zones or to supplement the full-time military in undertaking combat or support missions.

The transition to an all-volunteer force dramatically affected military recruitment efforts. Enhanced educational benefits were offered to potential recruits as incentives to join the active-duty military, the National Guard, and the reserves. For National Guard and reserve force members, using educational benefits to fund full-time study while concurrently serving as a member of the military represents a feasible and attractive option (Asch and Loughran, 2004). ROTC programs also offer educational support for students in exchange for active-duty service and commissioning as officers upon graduation. ROTC membership and its educational benefits are now an option for some nontraditional students, graduate students, and individuals who have previously earned undergraduate degrees (National Institute of Standards and Technology, 1996). In addition, ROTC cadets may affiliate concurrently with a National Guard or reserve unit via the Simultaneous Membership Program, and in many cases, the educational benefits available are higher when they do so (Wan, 2003). National Guard and reserve units, including their student members, can be activated and deployed often with very little advance notice and no consideration of academic schedules, deadlines, or students' enrollment status.

Deployment Patterns and Implications for College Enrollment

Although the 1991 Persian Gulf War, Operation Desert Storm, was brief in duration, it involved large-scale activations and deployments of National Guard and reserve troops to augment full-time military forces. Press reports of student members of the National Guard and reserves who withdrew from college in response to activation (for example, Collison, 1991; Dodge, 1991) documented the same kinds of enrollment discontinuity patterns that characterize contemporary student soldiers' experiences. Campus officials began to implement policies and accommodations for students who faced withdrawal from college (see Chapter Six), and related federal provisions—for example, extending Pell Grant eligibility and student loan deferment periods for deployed students—were enacted (DeLoughry, 1991).

The current "War on Terror"—a blanket term that covers a number of military actions, including Operation Noble Eagle, Operation Enduring Freedom, and Operation Iraqi Freedom—has involved large numbers of National Guard and reserve unit activations. Many of the National Guard and reserve personnel were in college at the time of their activation, and subsequent deployments have interrupted their college enrollment for a year or longer. Relatively unpredictable departures, complicated by extended deployment periods, have interrupted students' academic career. When activated, these students experience an accelerated transition to active-duty service, moving quickly from the college campus to expedited training and then to service at bases or in combat zones overseas.

According to John Mikelson, director of distance learning for Student Veterans of America and veterans advisor at the University of Iowa, services provided to student servicemembers who have been activated or are returning from a deployment varies from institution to institution and depends largely on the state where the college or university is located (John Mikelson, personal communication, March 24, 2009). State governing agencies likely determine procedures for institutions to follow. Moreover, higher education organizations may also make recommendations for working with student veterans (see Servicemembers Opportunity Colleges, 2005, for examples). At present, there are no consistent policies and procedures for colleges and universities to follow.

Student veterans frequently re-enroll or enter college following active duty, and college and university officials need to be prepared to help ease their transition. The myriad issues that student veterans face include academic re-entry, contractual and financial matters, and needs for advising and counseling assistance. Although offices that provide services and support exist on most campuses already, particular services may require tailoring to address the specific needs of students who are or were members of the military. For example, upon deactivation, a veteran's college or university re-entry can be delayed by the need to wait for an upcoming academic term to begin. This scenario may be exacerbated by unresolved problems associated with departures at off times—for example, the need to make up exams, reinstate insurance coverage, or adjust financial aid packages (Rumann and Hamrick, 2007). Transitions for returning veterans can be difficult as well. And because National Guard and reserve units are subject to reactivations and redeployments, upon their return, individuals may need to negotiate simultaneous statuses as veterans, servicemembers, and students (see Chapter Two). A number of campuses have instituted proactive services and transitional supports so that the responsibility for a successful transition need not fall to the returning individual alone. Other chapters in this volume describe examples of such services and programs.

Relevant Campus Considerations

Anticipating the influx of World War II veterans into colleges and universities, Washton (1945) recommended that counselors or advisors for veterans be appointed from the ranks of professors who were themselves military veterans. He further recommended that professors who teach veterans have "a sympathetic understanding of the soldier and the soldier's experiences in all parts of the world" (p. 196). Ideally, campus professionals, including faculty and student affairs administrators, who work with today's student veterans would also possess such experiences and understandings.

From generational and societal perspectives, large numbers of current administrators and faculty members have likely not experienced military or wartime service. World War II veterans are virtually all retired or deceased. Also, during the Vietnam War era, it was relatively common for college men to obtain educational deferments that permitted continued enrollment in graduate school and advanced degree programs. And although higher education and the U.S. military share a long history of preparing servicemembers and educating veterans, it is more likely that current administrators and faculty members are well intentioned but have few or no firsthand experiences with military culture—save individuals with National Guard or reserves affiliations—or within combat zones as military personnel. Student veterans often face complicated situations—such as working through confusing or perplexing expectations in regard to personal and social roles; resolving unpredictable disruptions of their good standing with respect to eligibility for services or financial assistance; negotiating, ending, or initiating personal relationships; locating or creating comfortable and supportive environments; or resuming their life as a student—frequently with greater seriousness of purpose than the student population at large (Rumann and Hamrick, 2007). If veterans are not well represented among campus faculty members and administrators, and if these individuals have little firsthand or systematic knowledge of military culture and the potential impact of wartime service on servicemembers, it may complicate campus efforts to serve student veterans and facilitate successful transitions for veterans. Indeed, DiRamio, Ackerman, and Mitchell's respondents reported facing anti-military bias on their campuses, particularly among faculty members (DiRamio, Ackerman, and Mitchell, 2008). For example, the findings of their study indicated that some professors made inappropriate disclosure requests of student veterans in class or regarded student veterans as spokespersons for all veterans, both of which echo the marginalizing dynamic of regarding African American students as convenient if not also authoritative spokespersons for all African Americans (Davis and others, 2004).

External Partnerships. For the reasons just discussed, it may be fruitful for higher education institutions to partner with veterans organizations, local National Guard or reserve personnel, or community organizations in designing and providing services for student veterans (see Chapter Seven). Campus partnerships or collaborations with veterans services and veterans organizations as well as local military units honor the multiple roles of student, veteran, and servicemember that returning military personnel simultaneously experience. Student veterans frequently seek contacts with other veterans and military personnel as ways to validate their experiences and aid in successfully making the transition to college (DiRamio, Ackerman, and Mitchell, 2008; Rumann and Hamrick, 2007), and it would be relatively easy for campuses to initiate such partnerships in order to make contacts readily available to students. It may be tempting to support a model of separate spheres in which, for example, the local Veterans Administration office handles the "servicemember" or "veteran" issues while the college handles the "student" issues. However, such a model is not consistent with transition processes that at some level aim to integrate and reconcile a student's various roles and experiences rather than separate or compartmentalize the sets of experiences, social roles, and, ultimately, personal identities (Rumann and Hamrick, 2007). ROTC programs may provide support and appropriate environments for many student servicemembers and veterans, but the specific career path and level of commitment entailed by ROTC membership may at best partially address needs for affirmation and support among student veterans who have decided not to enter the military as a career.

Building Awareness. Campus administrators, including student affairs and academic affairs leaders, can provide students, staff members, and faculty with opportunities to better understand the kinds of military experiences that may be absent from their own set of experiences or knowledge base. Indeed, learning about the military, war and combat, and servicemembers' experiences could complement a campus's broader commitment to diversity and social understanding. For example, Noddings (2004) recommended exploring psychological issues related to war as a powerful way to foster critical thinking about topics such as gender, class, and socialization. Political science, history, and military science departments may already offer credit-bearing courses on political and military history, military tactics, or topics related to war and peace. Administrators should also focus on developing educational opportunities to explore human-level experiences in and of war (see, for example, Foster, 2005), or read related works of fiction or memoirs. For example, Tim O'Brien's *The Things They Carried* or Anthony Swofford's *Jarhead* offer accounts of combat experiences in Vietnam and Iraq (O'Brien, 1990; Swofford, 2005). Ha Jin's *War Trash* (2005) and *Ocean of Words* (1996) describe combat and personal experiences during the war in China between Communist and Nationalist forces. In addition, student veterans themselves or military representatives can be invited to present perspectives on relevant topics. In-service training for student affairs professionals is also recommended; perhaps student veterans and military or veterans representatives can be engaged to discuss a range of needs and perspectives with counseling center staff members, academic advisors, and personnel in areas such as student activities, financial aid, or student health. These types of studies, discussions, or in-service sessions may result in larger considerations of war and peace, foreign policy, or warranted (if at all) use of armed force, but we recommend these opportunities primarily as ways for campus professionals to become familiar on some level with a set of experiences that is increasingly common among a growing number of students. This new knowledge can help provide essential perspectives to individuals who design, implement, or adapt services and programs for student veterans.

Conclusions and Recommendations

Raising awareness of the experiences and needs of student veterans is the first step toward promoting and developing effective support services. On many campuses, responsibility for meeting student veterans' needs is frequently assigned to the designated veterans representatives. These individuals undoubtedly play critical roles in successful transition processes.

NEW DIRECTIONS FOR STUDENT SERVICES • DOI: 10.1002/ss

However, it is increasingly apparent that the needs of veterans in transition frequently extend beyond assembling required documentation and ensuring that educational benefits are accessed; moreover, veterans representatives may quickly become overextended as the numbers of student veterans grow and as GI Bill and related educational benefit guidelines continue to develop in complexity. The servicemember and veteran roles accompany military personnel back to campus; thus, campuswide efforts—in partnership with external organizations and agencies—are best positioned to help student veterans make successful transitions. Proactive steps should also be taken so that student veterans have easy access to support information and are aware of the services available to them. Such steps should include, for example, links for veterans on institutional Web sites and contact information for the student-led veterans organization on campus, if one exists.

Based on the long shared history of higher education and the military in the United States and grounded in more recent military personnel practices, deployment trends, and financial assistance for college, the presence of student veterans on campuses is likely to grow. As this chapter has demonstrated, student veteran transitions are not a new development in U.S. higher education. However, given an all-volunteer military force that includes members of the National Guard and reserves, the roles of student, servicemember, and veteran have become less clear-cut and bounded and are often experienced simultaneously as well as sequentially. Traditional separations and segmentations into veterans services (for example, Veterans Administration benefits advising) and academic services (for example, course advising) appear to be less appropriate than partnerships that honor student veterans' perspectives, spanning and integrating their roles as student, veteran, and servicemember. To that end, we suggest establishing proactive and working partnerships to help create a more seamless environment for students who need to successfully navigate multiple agencies, organizations, and bureaucracies and to help create or find supportive individuals and environments to facilitate the transitions of student veterans.

The organizations, agencies, and individuals that represent potential partners—for example, the Veterans Administration, Veterans of Foreign Wars, or National Guard or reserve personnel—may also be consulted to determine how to best serve the emerging population of student veterans as they make transitions into and out of active-duty status and into and out of college. Colleges and universities should take the first steps to initiate contacts and explore partnership possibilities through meetings and discussions involving multiple parties. Finally, it is important to learn from and follow the lead of the current group of student servicemembers and student veterans and to treat them as pioneers and invaluable sources of information on their own experiences, concerns, and questions.

NEW DIRECTIONS FOR STUDENT SERVICES • DOI: 10.1002/ss

References

Abrams, R. M. "The U.S. Military and Higher Education: A Brief History." *Annals of the American Academy of Political and Social Science*, 1989, *502*, 15–28.

Army National Guard. "About Us." [http://www.arng.army.mil/AboutUs.aspx]. 2008. Retrieved June 23, 2008.

Asch, B. J., Fair, C. C., and Kilburn, M. R. *An Assessment of Recent Proposals to Improve the Montgomery G.I. Bill.* Santa Monica, Calif.: RAND, 2000.

Asch, B. J., Kilburn, M. R., and Klerman, J. A. *Attracting College-Bound Youth into the Military: Toward the Development of New Recruiting Policy Options.* Santa Monica, Calif.: RAND, 1999.

Asch, B. J., and Loughran, D. *Reserve Recruiting and the College Market.* Santa Monica, Calif.: RAND, 2004.

Collison, M. "Black Students Have Mixed Views on Gulf War." *Chronicle of Higher Education.* [http://chronicle.com/che-data/articles.dir/articles-37.dir/issue-21.dir/21a02902.htm]. Feb. 6, 1991. Retrieved June 5, 2008.

Davis, M., Dias-Bowie, Y., Greenberg, K., Klukken, G., Pollio, H. R., Thomas, S. P., and Thompson, C. L. "'A Fly in the Buttermilk': Descriptions of University Life by Successful Black Undergraduates at a Predominantly White Southeastern University." *Journal of Higher Education*, 2004, *75*(4), 420–445.

DeLoughry, T. J. "Repeal Backed on Test Requirements for Students Lacking School Diplomas." *Chronicle of Higher Education.* [http://chronicle.com/che-data/articles.dir/articles-37.dir/issue-27.dir/27a03101.htm]. Mar. 20, 1991. Retrieved July 15, 2008.

DiRamio, D., Ackerman, R., and Mitchell, R. L. "From Combat to Campus: Voices of Student-Veterans." *NASPA Journal*, 2008, *45*(1), 73–102.

Dodge, S. "Thousands of College Students Protest Persian Gulf War in Rallies and Sit-Ins; Others Support Military Action." *Chronicle of Higher Education.* [http://chronicle.com/che-data/articles.dir/articles-37.dir/issue-20.dir/20a02801.htm]. Jan. 30, 1991. Retrieved June 5, 2008.

Doubler, M. D., and Listman, J. W. *The National Guard: An Illustrated History of America's Citizen-Soldiers.* (2nd ed.) Washington, D.C.: Potomac Books, 2007.

Foster, A. "Swarthmore Radio Show Airs Voices of Iraqis and U.S. Soldiers." *Chronicle of Higher Education.* [http://chronicle.com/weekly/v52/i14/14a04201.htm]. Nov. 25, 2005. Retrieved June 5, 2008.

Gruber, C. S. *Mars and Minerva: World War I and the Uses of the Higher Learning in America.* Baton Rouge, La.: Louisiana State University Press, 1975.

Horan, M. *Stepchildren of Archaoes: An Ethnography of a Support Group for Vietnam Veterans at the Florida State University Campus.* 1990. (ED 347 331)

Jin, H. *Ocean of Words: Army Stories.* Cambridge, Mass.: Zoland Books, 1996.

Jin, H. *War Trash.* New York: Vintage, 2005.

Military.com. "New GI Bill Overview." [http://education.military.com/money-for-school/gi-bill/new-gi-bill-overview]. 2008. Retrieved July 13, 2008.

National Institute of Standards and Technology. "National Defense Authorization Act for Fiscal Year 1996." [http://www.nist.gov/director/ocla/Public_Laws/PL104–106.pdf]. 1996. Retrieved July 11, 2008.

Neiberg, M. S. *Making Citizen-Soldiers: ROTC and the Ideology of American Military Service.* Cambridge, Mass.: Harvard University Press, 2000.

Noddings, N. "War, Critical Thinking, and Self-Understanding." *Phi Delta Kappan*, 2004, *85*(7), 489–495.

O'Brien, T. *The Things They Carried.* Boston: Houghton Mifflin, 1990.

Olson, K. W. *The G.I. Bill, the Veterans, and the Colleges.* Lexington, Ky.: University Press of Kentucky, 1974.

Rumann, C. B., and Hamrick, F. A. "Student Soldiers: Returning from a War Zone." Paper presented at the joint meeting of the National Association for Student Personnel Administrators and ACPA–College Student Educators International, Orlando, Fla., April 3, 2007.

Servicemembers Opportunity Colleges. "Policy Letters, Federal Law, State Laws, and Governance Policies." [http://www.soc.aascu.org/socguard/PolicyLetters.html]. 2005. Retrieved July 11, 2008.

Smith, D. C., Jr. "To Protect a Free Society: Maintaining Excellence in the Military." *Educational Record*, 1985, *66*(1), 10–13.

Swofford, A. *Jarhead: A Marine's Chronicle of the Gulf War and Other Battles*. New York: Simon & Schuster/Pocket Books, 2005.

Toven, J. R. "College Counseling for the War Veteran." *Journal of Educational Sociology*, 1945, *18*(6), 331–339.

United States Army Reserve. "People." [http://www.armyreserve.army.mil/ARWEB/ORGANIZATION/PEOPLE/Soldiers.htm]. 2008. Retrieved June 23, 2008.

Wan, W. "ROTC Ranks Swelling on Campus; Recruiters Cite Iraq War, Financial Incentives as Reasons." *Washington Post*, Aug. 28, 2003, p. 3.

Washton, N. S. "A Veteran Goes to College." *Journal of Higher Education*, 1945, *16*(4), 195–196, 226.

COREY B. RUMANN *is a doctoral candidate in the Department of Educational Leadership and Policy Studies at Iowa State University.*

FLORENCE A. HAMRICK *is associate professor of higher education in the Department of Educational Leadership and Policy Studies at Iowa State University.*

NEW DIRECTIONS FOR STUDENT SERVICES • DOI: 10.1002/ss

The number of women veterans attending college is increasing. Campus professionals need to be aware of how issues pertaining to mental health, sexual assault, and gender identity may influence how these women make transitions to higher education.

Meeting the Needs of Women Veterans

Margaret Baechtold, Danielle M. De Sawal

Just as veterans are an increasing segment of our student population, women are becoming a larger proportion of the veteran population. The demographics of the United States' active-duty military force have shifted dramatically over the past twenty-five years, especially in regard to gender. In 1973, women made up only 2.5 percent of the total active-duty force, but by 2005, the number had increased fourfold, bringing the total to approximately 14 percent (U.S. Department of Veterans Affairs, 2007). In addition, the recent rise in the total number of female personnel serving on the front lines of two wars is placing women in new roles, both as members of the military and as veterans. Media reports indicate that approximately 11 percent of U.S. troops deployed to Iraq or Afghanistan are women, and a total of more than 182,000 have served there since these conflicts began. This is a historic increase in women who have been deployed to combat zones. In comparison, during the Vietnam conflict, roughly 7,500 women were deployed, primarily as nurses. Changes in assignment policies for women increased that number to 41,000 in a wide range of career fields during the Gulf War (Stone, 2008).

Not only have the numbers of women in the military increased, but their exposure to the stresses of war has increased as their location in combat zones has changed. Formally, the policy of the military is that women are to be excluded from assignment to combat arms units, but the lines between combat and noncombat missions in the current conflicts are frequently almost nonexistent (Baker, 2006). In modern combat operations, support units are as susceptible to attack as frontline units, with "no safe

place and no safe duty" (Litz, n.d., p. 1). In combat, "women are co-located with ground combat units. These women are providing convoy security; they are leading convoys in, to, and through ground combat as well as patrolling main supply routes" (Baker, 2006, p. 10). As a result, women are as exposed to the dangers of war as men and are subject to the same stresses and mental health concerns (Stone, 2008). The increase in the number of women enrolling in postsecondary education following their tour of duty suggests that campus professionals need to become aware of how issues associated with mental health, sexual assault, and gender identity may influence how women veterans make the transition into the higher education environment. This chapter addresses the special needs of women veterans.

Mental Health Problems

Mental health issues on college campuses have received increased attention over the past several years as a result of the shootings at Virginia Tech and Northeastern Illinois University. The mental health concerns associated with military service and combat are often understood by society through the personal stories that veterans share. This view could lead those not familiar with military-related health issues to conclude that these problems are common among veterans. The reality is that a moderate percentage of veterans are diagnosed with mental health issues, according to the National Center for Posttraumatic Stress Disorder (n.d.). However, student affairs administrators need to be aware that returning combat veterans need a safe place in order to process their war-related experiences.

Post-Traumatic Stress Disorder. The connection between post-traumatic stress disorder (PTSD) and military veterans has been acknowledged for many years. The estimated risk of suffering from PTSD is approximately 18 percent after service in Iraq and 11 percent after service in Afghanistan (Litz, n.d.). While the percentage of veterans who are expected to be diagnosed with PTSD is moderate, many others will have experiences that will require support to process. Student affairs personnel need to be prepared to assist veterans who come to campus with experiences that are not common in the traditional college student. Student veterans will likely require time and support in a nonthreatening environment to process their experiences, especially with peers who are veterans and who understand what it means to be deployed to a war zone. Advances in medical and military technology have made the survival rate in combat historically high. This fact creates a situation in which soldiers are much more likely to witness or suffer from the "aftermath of violence" (Litz, n.d., p. 2). Although they might not be diagnosed with PTSD, many veterans today have seen their peers severely injured, witnessed death, and experienced grief.

The Department of Defense Task Force on Mental Health reports that "female servicemembers in combatant areas have had to fight the enemy in the same manner as their male counterparts: engaging in firefights, taking prisoners, and occasionally becoming casualties" (U.S. Department of Defense, 2007, p. 58). The current conflicts in Iraq and Afghanistan "are the first combat operations where a large number of female service personnel have had the potential for repeated exposures to combat situations. Repeat deployments have also added to the exposure potential" (U.S. Department of Defense, 2007, p. 58). The report cites conflicting findings from studies on the psychological effects of combat on women. Reports indicate that female veterans are more likely than their male counterparts to suffer from PTSD. This is also true within the general population, in which women suffer from PTSD at a rate twice as high as men (Perconte and others, 1993; Dobie and others, 2004). However, women are not as likely to be diagnosed with PTSD as men are. The authors of the Department of Defense report theorize that this may be based on cultural views that do not easily recognize women as combatants, as well as a tendency to diagnose women's mental health problems as depression or anxiety rather than combat-related PTSD (U.S. Department of Defense, 2007). Added to these factors is a tendency for women to not define themselves as veterans after they have completed their service, coupled with women's concern about maintaining the emotional and psychological strength expected of military members (U.S. Department of Defense, 2007). These issues can create barriers that prevent women from seeking treatment.

Throughout their deployment, military personnel experience the daily stress associated with combat readiness. Although technological advances have made it possible for military personnel to remain connected with their family while at war, servicemembers often find the combination of home and combat difficult to balance. They learn to compartmentalize their lives, bringing family and relationships to the forefront only when it feels safe and they can handle the merging of these two worlds. This phenomenon may carry over after separation from the military.

When women veterans share anecdotal stories that describe their frustration with returning to civilian life, they offer opportunities to understand their transitions. The day-to-day dramas and crises that plague the typical civilian woman may appear ridiculous and absurd when compared with the dangers of combat (Blankenship, 2008). Therefore, student affairs personnel need to be aware that the typical situations that are stressful or difficult for traditional college women likely will not affect women veterans in the same manner. This realization means understanding that how women veterans process and make meaning of their college experience will be influenced by how they are making meaning of their combat experiences.

Sexual Assault. *Military sexual trauma* is the term used to describe any sexual harassment or sexual assault that occurs in the military. While data specific to veterans of the current conflicts are unavailable, the U.S. Department of Veterans Affairs revealed that among veterans who sought health care through the Veterans Administration, 23 percent of women reported sexual assault while in the military and 55 percent reported some form of sexual harassment (National Center for Posttraumatic Stress Disorder, 2007). While there are numerous statistics related to unwanted sexual conduct available, comparisons are difficult because the definitions used can include rape, sexual assault, sexual harassment, or any combination of the three categories. Findings from the "Department of Defense FY07 Report on Sexual Assault in the Military" revealed that 6.8 percent of women in the military reported unwanted sexual conduct (U.S. Department of Defense, 2008). Army statistics reported a much lower incidence of unwanted sexual conduct in the forward operating areas of Iraq and Afghanistan than in the Army at large, and that finding is attributed to high levels of unit cohesion in combat zones and tight restriction of alcohol consumption (Ryan, 2008). An additional study found that 78 percent of women experienced sexual harassment on active duty, while 6 percent had experienced rape (Vogt, n.d., p. 3).

Skinner and others (2000) discuss the specific impacts of sexual harassment or assault on military women. Feelings of loneliness and being left out were common adjustment issues reported upon return to civilian life by female military personnel who had experienced sexual assault. These women were likely to feel that their experiences would not be understood by their family and their peers. Anxiety, substance abuse, depression, and anger were all common reactions during readjustment (Skinner and others, 2000). Among those who reported military-related sexual assault, instances of depression were three times higher and incidents of alcohol abuse two times higher than among those who did not experience assault (Hankin and others, 1999).

Student affairs personnel need to be aware of the mental health problems that might affect female veterans when they attend college but should not assume that all female veterans arrive on campus with these issues. Rather, while most of returning women veterans will not show signs of mental health issues, many will struggle with how to make the transition to civilian life, including their role as a college student. In essence, they need to make meaning of what they have seen and experienced while at war. The process of meaning making is related to the idea of shifting from accepting knowledge from an authority to constructing knowledge for oneself, based on individual learning and experiences (Baxter Magolda, 2001).

Understanding the Identity Development of Women Veterans

Student affairs professionals often use psychosocial and identity theories to understand how individuals view their personal and interpersonal lives during college (McEwen, 2003). Understanding the development of women veterans requires making a connection between what these women experienced during their military service and how those experiences may or may not relate to how they make meaning of their experiences as college students. The growing population of women veterans on campus creates the need for the development of a new framework for understanding how this student population views their collegiate experience. The reconceptualized model of multiple dimensions of identity (Abes, Jones, and McEwen, 2007) provides a framework for understanding the contextual influences that affect women veterans. The voices of military personnel are captured through anecdotal stories in the popular press or through limited studies conducted through the military branches, revealing that the context of the military is distinctly different from that of higher education. Moreover, the societal expectations that accompany experiences in the military and in higher education are also distinctly different. The multiple cognitive, intrapersonal, and interpersonal dimensions that influence how women veterans make meaning of their military experiences do not always connect with how they view themselves or how others on campus view them. This is especially true because few of their civilian peers can relate to what it means to be in the military. Abes, Jones, and McEwen (2007) state that a "key consideration in understanding students' multiple identities is for student affairs professionals to acknowledge and understand the nature of contextualinfluences" (pp. 19–20). Student affairs administrators have the opportunity to engage students in discussions that could begin to bridge that contextual gap.

Life in the military is very different from what is experienced by the average freshman in college. Although freshmen may experience certain benchmarks as they learn to be more independent and establish an identity, colleges do not train students in the way that the military trains soldiers. An individual's introduction to military life occurs during basic training, in which the mental and physical demands are significantly different from those placed on first-year students in college. Herbert (1998) stated, "The process of basic training is one of depersonalization and deindividuation in which the military, in the form of drill sergeants, must strip the individual of all previous self-definition . . . [B]asic training . . . is also intended to vest each participant with a clear notion of what it means to be a soldier, a Marine, and so forth. In the case of military training, these images are characteristically male" (p. 9). She further noted, "Women who enter a male-dominant setting must learn how to redefine and manage 'femaleness'" (Herbert, 1998, p. 21). Herbert asserted that women in the military feel pressures to act either more feminine, more masculine, or both. Some women react by playing up their femininity through their attire, makeup, and surroundings. Others suppress their femininity or engage in more typically male behaviors such as swearing or drinking alcohol. Herbert also reported that women are often reluctant to allow others, especially men, to help them, even in circumstances where help is warranted, for fear of appearing weak. This reluctance to accept help was true for tasks that required physical strength as well as in other tasks that occurred during both training and service. In these cases, strategies were employed that often moved the individual away from natural expression of gender to a more forced and conscious one. This learning may be difficult to counteract upon return to civilian life. Herbert's study was completed during peacetime, and it is likely that these pressures are even more prevalent in wartime.

The psychosocial outcomes of basic training as just described do not easily fit into the models of identity development that are related to traditional college students. Although it addresses specific components of Chickering and Reisser's (1993) "seven vectors," basic training forces servicemembers into a pre-assigned identity that, in most cases, is highly valued only within the military community. As a result, when the structured military community is removed, the individual is forced to again redefine who she is as a civilian, a veteran, a female, and a student. In regard to gender development, the identity that was respected in the military is one that demonstrates male characteristics. Therefore, when women veterans re-enter civilian life, they are often unsure of how to fulfill not only their specific role as a student but also their role as a woman. The gender issue is distinctly different for men because they are often rewarded by society for displaying strong male characteristics.

Women veterans face other unique challenges as they return to civilian life and attend college. As Herbert (1998) reported, women in the military are forced into a more conscious and deliberate role as an armed force member and are not allowed a natural expression of gender. Through the work of Marcia, we understand that identity development occurs along two dimensions: (1) an awareness that an identity crisis exists and must be resolved and (2) the commitment to an identity (Marcia, 1966). Removal of the forced military identity causes a crisis of identity for female veterans as they struggle to re-assume roles as civilians.

Josselson (1987) explored how women develop a sense of self, mirroring the work of Marcia. Josselson would identify women veterans as "identity achievers" or "pavers of the way." These women have formed a distinct identity in which their occupation is an expression of who they are as an individual. When their military occupation is removed and a new vocation must be found in a college or university setting, many women veterans face a unique identity crisis. The way in which they constructed meaning for their life is not appreciated on campus as it was in the military. As a result of this dissonance, women veterans need to socially construct a new identity that is specifically related to gender in order to make meaning of the collegiate environment.

Finally, the transitions that male veterans face when enrolling in college are likely facilitated by the presence on campus of male veterans among faculty and staff (see Chapter Two and Chapter Eight). Female veterans on campus are less likely than male veterans to find same-gender role models. In addition, while serving in the military, females had fewer same-gender role models than males did. When women veterans come to campus and face issues associated with establishing an identity, they will need to be able to find other women with whom to connect.

Suggestions for Practitioners

Working with women students who are veterans ideally involves an understanding of both gender identity issues and the transitions associated with moving from the role of active military member to that of a civilian college student. Understanding the specific issues associated with female veterans requires student affairs personnel to be aware of the multiple dimensions of identify development. These women likely need to make meaning of both their past and their present context. Gaining an understanding of how women veterans filter and process meaning making related to identity formation will provide student affairs professionals with a way to "effectively see [these] students as they see themselves by understanding not only *what* they perceive their identity to be, but also *how* they make meaning of their identity dimensions as they do, how they come to perceive identity dimensions as salient or relatively unimportant, and to what degree they understand their social identities as integrated or distinct" (Abes, Jones, and McEwen, 2007, p. 19). The challenge for student affairs professionals is to understand and value the experiences of women veterans so that they can be helped to define their sense of self in relation to the college campus and their civilian status.

As discussed elsewhere in this volume, campus leaders have responded to the growing number of student veterans by providing services to support that population. Student veteran centers, peer advising, orientation programs for veterans, and student veterans organizations are examples of the supportive initiatives that have been deemed helpful by veterans as well as by higher education leaders (Redden, 2008). Faculty and staff, especially student affairs educators who seek to support female veterans as they make the transition from combat to classroom, should consider the following topics in their discussions with students.

- What steps might you take to connect with other military veterans who are students on this campus?
- How might you begin making connections with other women on this campus?
- To what extent are you aware of the support services available to students?
- What are the sources of your stress as a student, as a female, and as a veteran?

Questions that focus on specific combat experiences may be difficult for veterans to answer. Many students may ask veterans these questions out of curiosity and not realize that the questions may evoke emotions or experiences that these students are still processing. When working with veterans on campus, it is best to avoid questions that directly relate to combat, including questions about having to kill another human being, having been shot or wounded, or having observed others in these situations.

NEW DIRECTIONS FOR STUDENT SERVICES • DOI: 10.1002/ss

Further Research

Women veterans' needs on college campuses should be explored further through research. The majority of literature related to understanding a woman's experience in the military comes from the popular press and military reports. Most of these sources of information focus more on providing personal stories than on presenting empirical research findings. Moreover, neither military training exercises nor the realities of being on the front lines of war are considered in any of the current models or theories associated with women's development. An area of importance to higher education researchers and student affairs professionals is how military service affects gender development in women student veterans, a topic we touched on in this chapter.

As more women veterans enroll in college, practitioners should be aware of the unique needs of these students as they participate in all aspects of campus life. Directly related to this need for awareness on the part of educators is the need to help students who do not have military experience understand and appreciate this student population. How these conversations can best be approached in a manner that builds community and understanding needs to be explored.

References

Abes, E. S., Jones, S. R., and McEwen, M. K. "Reconceptualizing the Model of Multiple Dimensions of Identity: The Role of Meaning-Making Capacity in the Construction of Multiple Identities." *Journal of College Student Development,* 2007, *48*(1), 1–22.

Baker, H. *Women in Combat: A Culture Issue?* Carlisle Barracks, Pa.: U.S. Army War College Strategy Research Project, U.S. Army War College, 2006.

Baxter Magolda, M. B. *Making Their Own Way: Narratives for Transforming Higher Education to Promote Self-Development.* Sterling, Va.: Stylus, 2001.

Blankenship, J. "Women in Today's Military Are Paving New Paths." *VFW Magazine,* 2008, *95*(7), 14–18.

Chickering, A. W., and Reisser, L. *Education and Identity.* (2nd ed.) San Francisco: Jossey-Bass, 1993.

Dobie, D., Kivlahan, D., Maynard, C., Bush, K., Davis, T., and Bradley, K. "Posttraumatic Stress Disorder in Female Veterans: Association with Self-Reported Health Problems and Functional Impairment." *Archives of Internal Medicine.* [http://www.archinternmed.com]. 2004. Retrieved Nov. 8, 2007.

Hankin, C. S., Skinner, K. M., Sullivan, L. M., Miller, D. R., Frayne, S., and Tripp, T. J. "Prevalence of Depressive and Alcohol Abuse Symptoms Among Women VA Outpatients Who Report Experiencing Sexual Assault While in the Military." *Journal of Traumatic Stress,* 1999, *12*(4), 601–612.

Herbert, M. S. *Camouflage Isn't Only for Combat: Gender, Sexuality, and Women in the Military.* New York: New York University Press, 1998.

Josselson, R. *Finding Herself: Pathways to Identity Development in Women.* San Francisco: Jossey-Bass, 1987.

Litz, B. T. "The Unique Circumstance and Mental Health Impact of the Wars in Afghanistan and Iraq." [http://www.ncptsd.va.gov/ncmain/ncdocs/fact_shts/fs_iraqafghanistan_wars.html]. n.d. Retrieved Nov. 8, 2007.

Marcia, J. E. "Development and Validation of Ego Status. *Journal of Personality and Social Psychology,* 1966, *3,* 551–558.

McEwen, M. K. "The Nature and Uses of Theory." In S. R. Komives and D. B. Woodard, Jr. (eds.), *Student Services: A Handbook for the Profession*. (4th ed.) San Francisco: Jossey-Bass, 2003.

National Center for Posttraumatic Stress Disorder. "Fact Sheet: An Overview of the Mental Health Effects of Serving in Afghanistan and Iraq." [http://www.ncptsd.va.gov/ncmain/ncdocs/fact_shts/overview_mental_health_effects.html]. n.d. Retrieved Nov. 8, 2007.

Perconte, S. T., Wilson, A. T., Pontius, E. B., Deitrick, A. L., and Spiro, K. J. "Psychological and War Stress Symptoms Among Deployed and Non-Deployed Reservists Following the Persian Gulf War." *Military Medicine*, 1993, *158*(8), 516–521.

Redden, E. "Operation Transition." [www.insidehighered.com/news/2008/-7/10/veterans]. 2008. Retrieved July 10, 2008.

Ryan, D. "DoD Releases Sexual Assault Report." [http://www.army.mil/-news/2008/03/18/7982-dod-releases-sexual-assault-report/]. 2008. Retrieved Mar. 26, 2008.

Skinner, K. M., Kressin, N., Frayne, S., Tripp, T. J., Hankin, C. S., and Miller, D. R. "The Prevalence of Military Sexual Assault Among Female Veterans' Administration Outpatients." *Journal of Interpersonal Violence*, 2000, *15*, 291–310.

Stone, A. "Mental Toll of War Hitting Female Servicemembers." *USA Today*. [http://usatoday.com/news/nation/2008–01–01-womenvets_n.htm?POE=click-refer]. Jan.1, 2008. Retrieved Jan. 7, 2008.

U.S. Department of Defense. *An Achievable Vision: Report of the Department of Defense Task Force on Mental Health*. Falls Church, Va.: Defense Health Board, 2007.

U.S. Department of Defense. "Department of Defense FY07 Report on Sexual Assault in the Military." [http://www.sapr.mil/contents/references/2007%20Annual%20Report.pdf]. 2008. Retrieved July 25, 2008.

U.S. Department of Veterans Affairs. *Women Veterans: Past, Present and Future*. Washington D.C.: U.S. Department of Veterans Affairs, 2007.

Vogt, D. "Research on Women, Trauma and PTSD." [www.ncptsd.va.gov/ncmain/ncdocs/fact_shts/fs_womenptsdprof.html]. n.d. Retrieved Nov. 8, 2007.

MARGARET BAECHTOLD *is director of veterans support services at Indiana University and a retired military officer.*

DANIELLE M. DE SAWAL *is a clinical assistant professor and coordinator of the higher education and student affairs master's degree programs at Indiana University.*

5

This chapter discusses a statewide response to the needs of veterans, military members, and their families. Specifically, it addresses the collaboration between Minnesota Department of Veterans Affairs-Higher Education Veterans Programs, St. Cloud State University, and a student veteran organization.

A Statewide Approach to Creating Veteran-Friendly Campuses

Jayne M. Lokken, Donald S. Pfeffer, James McAuley, Christopher Strong

One of the most consistent messages we hear from veterans on campus is the need for a strong sense of community and belonging (see Chapter One). St. Cloud State University (SCSU), part of the Minnesota State Colleges and Universities system (MnSCU), is collaborating with the Minnesota Department of Veterans Affairs (MDVA) and the SCSU Student Veterans Organization to help develop this community. The work of these three entities is designed to provide a seamless integration of services to veterans on campus. Personnel from MDVA–Higher Education Veterans Programs worked with staff and faculty on campus to help implement veteran-friendly policies and procedures for the entire state college and university system.

The term *veteran-friendly* refers to marked efforts made by individual campuses to identify and remove barriers to the educational goals of veterans, to create smooth transitions from military life to college life, and to provide information about available benefits and services. Addressing the needs of this unique student population required the joint efforts of MDVA, MnSCU, the University of Minnesota, private colleges, the Minnesota Office of Higher Education, the governor, and the legislature. In this chapter, we will discuss the background and response of SCSU and MDVA–Higher Education Veterans Programs to the needs of returning veterans for successful adjustment to and reintegration into campus life. For the purposes of this chapter, the term *veteran* refers to veterans, active-duty military personnel, and their families.

New Directions for Student Services, no. 126, Summer 2009 © Wiley Periodicals, Inc.
Published online in Wiley InterScience (www.interscience.wiley.com) • DOI: 10.1002/ss.315

45

It is unclear how many veterans returning from deployment are dealing with mental health problems; however, for most, there is a readjustment process that can be difficult and stressful. If stressors are not dealt with, they may develop into more severe stress reactions or mental health concerns. In addition, among military members, there are significant perceived barriers to seeking help with mental health issues (Hoge and others, 2004). Mental health problems, including post-traumatic stress disorder and depression, begin to appear over a period of time following a veteran's return from deployment, particularly in veterans who have been injured during combat (Grieger and others, 2006). The U.S. Department of Defense Task Force on Mental Health (2007) reported that 49 percent of National Guard members, 38 percent of Army soldiers, and 31 percent of Marines who have been in combat report symptoms of post-traumatic stress disorder, depression, or anxiety at 90 to 120 days after returning from war.

The high rate of self-reported stress-related problems of the National Guard members may be due to several factors, such as the disruption of their lives and their families' lives when they are deployed, living in a combat zone, and being sent directly home to their community after deployment rather than being returned to a base, where there are services available to deal with post-deployment issues that arise. According to two articles that discuss briefings by psychiatrist Colonel Richie on rising suicide rates in the Army, the most common cause of suicide is strained relationships; legal, financial, or occupational problems are identified as the second leading causes (Lorge, 2008; Mills, 2008). A multifaceted response of the military and civilian communities, including early intervention, strong social and practical support, and assistance in navigating bureaucratic procedures, can reduce the stigma associated with seeking help. Such a response can also reduce the risk that veterans will develop maladaptive responses in order to deal with losses sustained during and after combat.

Higher Education Initiative in Minnesota

There are no active-duty military installations in Minnesota. However, the Defense Manpower Data Center (cited in the Wisconsin Department of Veterans Affairs, 2008) reported that a higher percentage than the national average per state of Minnesota Army, Air Guard, and Army Reserve soldiers have been deployed into combat areas since September 11, 2001. In October 2005, approximately 2,600 Minnesota Army National Guard began preparing for deployment to Iraq as part of the Army's 1/34 Brigade Combat Team (BCT). During this period, the adjutant general of the Minnesota National Guard, Major General Larry Shellito, and Chaplain John Morris developed Beyond the Yellow Ribbon, a program to prepare families and communities for the anticipated homecoming in March 2007 of the largest contingent of Minnesota soldiers to return from combat since World War II.

NEW DIRECTIONS FOR STUDENT SERVICES • DOI: 10.1002/ss

Beyond the Yellow Ribbon was designed to prepare communities, including higher education institutions, to provide support to returning military members and their families. As part of this program, National Guard members are required to attend initial demobilization and then reintegration training 30 days, 60 days, and 90 days after returning from deployment. The program provides information about typical adjustment processes and identifies potential areas of concern as well as resources to help address those concerns. The community component of Beyond the Yellow Ribbon includes information about the role of higher education because of the significant number of education benefits now available to National Guard members (see Chapter Ten). The Higher Education Reintegration Training Team was formed to support the 1/34 BCT soldiers upon their arrival at their demobilization site. This team consisted of the state director and regional coordinators of the MDVA–Higher Education Veterans Programs, as well as staff from MnSCU's Office of the Chancellor and Office of Academic Affairs. The Higher Education Reintegration Training Team was formed to support the 1/34 BCT soldiers on their arrival at their demobilization site. This team consisted of the director and regional coordinators of the MDVA-Higher Education Veterans Programs, as well as staff from MnSCU's offices of the chancellor and academic affairs. The team conducted a survey of Minnesota soldiers within the 1/34 BCT and found that 79.8 percent planned to start or return to college (Pfeffer, 2007).

Staff from MnSCU's Office of the Chancellor played a major role in the development of the reintegration activities because the state system has a history of serving Minnesota Army National Guard (MNANG) members, dating back to 2003, when they developed "Guard On-line" for MNANG soldiers deployed to Bosnia (Minnesota State Colleges and Universities System, 2008a). MnSCU also played a major advocacy role, along with the Minnesota Department of Veterans Affairs, the University of Minnesota, the Minnesota Private College Council, the Minnesota Office of Higher Education, and the veterans community, in support of higher education legislation for veterans, military members, and their families.

Minnesota's Legislative Efforts in 2006

The Minnesota state legislature enacted higher education initiatives, including the appropriation of $600,000 to carry out the mandates of Minnesota Statute 197.585, the Higher Education Veterans Assistance Program. The statute mandates "central liaison staff and campus veterans assistance officers to provide information and assistance to veterans regarding the availability of state federal, local and private resources." The legislation also stated that "each campus of the University of Minnesota and each institution within the Minnesota State Colleges and Universities System *shall provide,* and each private college and university is *encouraged to provide,* adequate space for a veterans service office" (State of Minnesota, 2008a,

NEW DIRECTIONS FOR STUDENT SERVICES • DOI: 10.1002/ss

p. 1, italics added). In addition, the legislation required that the "Minnesota State Colleges and Universities System must recognize coursework and award educational credits for a veteran's military training and service, if the course or training meets the standards of the American Council of Education or equivalent. It encourages the University of Minnesota and private colleges and universities to do likewise" (State of Minnesota, 2008a, p. 1).

Another piece of legislation, Minnesota Statute 197.775 (Higher Education Fairness), directed MnSCU and the University of Minnesota "to treat all veterans as Minnesota residents for undergraduate tuition rate purposes, irrespective of their state of origin or residency" (State of Minnesota, 2008b, p. 1). Graduate students could also be considered residents if the person was a resident upon entering the military and begins a graduate program within two years of completing military service. Moreover, fairness legislation mandated that "University of Minnesota and Minnesota State Colleges and Universities System institutions may not assess late fees or other late charges for veterans who are eligible to receive, have applied for, and are waiting to receive federal educational assistance, nor prevent them from registering for a subsequent term" (State of Minnesota, 2008b, p. 1).

Minnesota's Legislative Efforts in 2007

The state legislature increased MDVA–Higher Education Veterans Programs funding from $600,000 to $1,050,000 annually. The legislature also created the "Minnesota GI Bill" (Minnesota Office of Higher Education, 2007) to provide tuition assistance for Minnesota veterans and members of the National Guard or reserves (with at least five years of continuous service) who have served on or after September 11, 2001, including some assistance for dependents. Beginning in July 2008, the program provides tuition benefits each semester if the cost of tuition exceeds an individual's financial support from federal student aid and federal military benefits. The benefit is capped at $3,000 per academic year and $10,000 lifetime.

Minnesota Department of Veterans Affairs–Higher Education Veterans Programs

In July 2006, the MDVA–Higher Education Veterans Programs began operation by dividing the state into six regions and assigning a coordinator in each region to carry out the mandates of the veterans assistance legislation. A program director was also hired to oversee the operation and the coordination efforts. At that time, there were three Minnesota higher education institutions providing some form of specialized programming for veterans, including centers for veterans, military members, and their families. By June 2007, forty-one campuses were operating veterans resource centers and serving more than 3,000 individuals. Students reported that the number one reason for using the centers was "conversation and connecting" with others who shared similar experiences and backgrounds. The purposes of the veterans resource centers include providing

- An environment in which veterans, military members, and their families feel welcome
- Information about services and resources
- Referrals to appropriate service providers
- Space for students to interact with others with similar backgrounds, experiences, and circumstances
- Support and encouragement for family members (Minnesota State Colleges and Universities System, 2008b)

Increased legislative funding for July 2007 allowed the program to increase the number of coordinators from six to twelve. In addition, the program director was able to hire a full-time administrative assistant. As of June 2008, fifty-six campus veterans resource centers have been established, and more than 4,000 individuals were served in the 2007–08 academic year.

In February 2007, the MDVA–Higher Education Veterans Programs partnered with Minnesota Online, an MnSCU call center, to develop an online information program on education benefits and services for military members. Since the call center began operation in May 2007, approximately 1,200 contacts have been made each month. The call center has phone operators on duty from 7 A.M. to 9 P.M. (Central time) Monday through Friday, and from 10 A.M. to 3 P.M. on Saturdays and Sundays. The service features live chat and frequently asked questions. The center receives calls from all parts of the world and has been able to provide answers to 98 percent of all questions within twenty-four hours. The center refers individuals to appropriate service providers and has a credentialed counselor to provide educational counseling services, including career counseling and advising. Individuals who need crisis services or mental health counseling are referred to appropriate services.

St. Cloud State University Veterans Services

In the spring of 2006, St. Cloud State University conducted a needs assessment and focus group of students who were active-duty military personnel or veterans, as well as their dependents. Results from both the needs assessment and the focus group revealed a need to

- Identify veterans on campus
- Provide communication mechanisms for veterans
- Provide opportunities to build a sense of community among veterans
- Assist veterans in navigating university processes, academic advising, and educational benefits

NEW DIRECTIONS FOR STUDENT SERVICES • DOI: 10.1002/ss

- Educate veterans about campus resources and procedures
- Enhance campus awareness of the presence of veterans and their reintegration process
- Promote a veteran-friendly environment

A second needs assessment was conducted in November 2007. This survey was sent via e-mail to all students who were using U.S. Department of Veterans Affairs (VA) educational benefits at St. Cloud State University. The survey was funded by the regional coordinator of MDVA–Higher Education Veterans Programs who was housed at SCSU. The twenty-one-question instrument was designed to measure student perspectives on university experiences that they viewed favorably, areas in which they had concerns, and what they would like implemented to improve the university's response to their particular needs. The Web-based survey was sent as an e-mail attachment, and the timeline for completion was two weeks.

The survey was sent to 380 students, and the response rate was 57 percent ($N = 215$). The current military status of respondents was 50 percent members of the National Guard or reserves, 24 percent veterans, 14 percent spouses or dependents, and 12 percent disabled veterans. Although students who are veterans receive financial support from various sources, nearly 75 percent cited the GI Bill as the main source of education funding, while others referred to loans (16 percent), employment (12 percent), and other (12 percent). Respondents were asked to rate campus services; the admissions office at SCSU scored the highest on satisfaction at 26.5 percent, and financial aid services scored lowest at 10 percent. The low score for financial aid services may have been due to the length of time it was taking for students to receive their GI Bill benefits, which are needed to pay initial tuition, rent, and books. At the beginning of the fall 2007 semester, it was taking eight to twelve weeks for the VA to process benefit payments. This problem was addressed through the Minnesota State Colleges and Universities system's Board of Trustees Policy 5.12: "The president or designee may grant short-term tuition and fee payment deferrals in cases where, due to exceptional circumstances, a student needs additional time to arrange third-party financing or otherwise satisfy a tuition and fee balance due. Deferrals must document the reason for and time duration of the deferral and must be signed by the president or designee" (Minnesota State Colleges and Universities System, 2007, p. 1). This policy had long been in effect but had not been applied to veterans.

When asked what areas respondents would like to have the university address (multiple responses were allowed), 57 percent requested financial guidance and resources, 45 percent asked for a larger veterans resource center, 40 percent wanted a veterans newsletter, 25 percent wanted medical services, 22 percent wanted a veterans support group, and 20 percent indicated a need for life management seminars. Sixty-four percent had completed the Free Application for Federal Student Aid (FAFSA); therefore, approximately

36 percent apparently did not file federal applications for financial aid. Moreover, only 50 percent had heard of the Minnesota GI Bill enacted in 2007. Fifty-eight percent had not visited the veterans resource center on campus. Seventy-seven percent stated that they would attend monthly luncheons at which the focus was benefits, employment, and financial aid. Sixty-six percent had not heard of the student veterans organization on campus. Interestingly, 13 percent rated SCSU as "very veteran friendly," 42 percent rated SCSU as "veteran friendly," 39 percent rated SCSU as "veteran neutral," and 6 percent rated SCSU as "veteran unfriendly."

Results of the survey were shared in the following semester with the SCSU president's Veterans Task Force, which was formed in the fall of 2007. The task force consisted of the director of counseling and psychological services, the director of career services, the director of admissions, the vice president for faculty relations, the director of financial aid, the registrar, the director of human resources, and the assistant director of student life and development. The task force also included a representative from each of the following departments: Atwood Memorial Union (the student union), Counseling and Psychological Services, Affirmative Action, the Business Office, and Student Disability Services. A faculty member from Information Media Services, a faculty member from Social Work, and three students who were veterans were also included as members of the task force. University leadership responded to the survey findings by identifying a larger space for the veterans resource center. Given the additional space, SCSU personnel plan to offer a veterans orientation, which will, among other topics important to veterans, provide information about financial resources and educational benefits. This orientation will include participation from groups such as the Veterans of Foreign Wars, the American Legion, Disabled Veterans of America, St. Cloud Veterans Affairs Medical Center, and the Minnesota Department of Employment and Economic Development. Additional satisfaction surveys will be conducted annually.

The results of the first needs assessment motivated campus personnel at St. Cloud State University to become one of the host sites for a regional coordinator of Minnesota Department of Veterans Affairs-Higher Education Veterans Programs. In addition, based on information from the spring 2006 needs assessment and focus group sessions, SCSU students, assisted by staff, started a student veterans organization and initiated a petition for a university-sponsored Web page, office space, and a full-time campus staff member to assist veterans. Within two weeks, students were able to obtain 500 signatures of support. Brown-bag lunch discussions were established in order to provide mechanisms for connection and community. An electronic mailing list was implemented in order to facilitate information dissemination and communication among veterans and interested community members. During the summer of 2006, a Web page was developed in order to inform students of events, campus resources, external resources, mentor programs, buddy programs, and stress busters programs, as well as to provide a point of contact for immediate answers to questions via e-mail provided by the regional coordinator of the MDVA-Higher Education Veterans Programs (St. Cloud State University, 2008).

St. Cloud State University's Student Veterans Organization

St. Cloud State University's Student Veterans Organization (SVO), one of ten organizations or clubs currently active on Minnesota college and university campuses, works closely with staff at the campus veterans resource center. The SVO focuses on three key objectives, all aimed at improving the lives of veterans: support, community, and advocacy (see Chapter Eight). The SVO augments the services provided by other veterans programs and functions as a transition mechanism for returning veterans who are making a shift back to civilian life. Families of military students and veterans can also use the SVO as a source of connection with other families who are dealing with transition issues.

One of the most significant results of the formation of St. Cloud State University's SVO is an increased awareness about educational benefits. Through conversation with members of the organization, SCSU students become informed about the benefits and opportunities available to them and pick up relevant information from fellow veterans based on past experiences and lessons learned. Members of the SVO serve as mentors or buddies for veterans who are new to college processes and experiences (St. Cloud State University, 2008).

A second benefit of the SVO is the emergence of a special community in which veterans and their family members can come together with others who share similar experiences and backgrounds. This community creates a sense of belonging, familiarity, and safety, enhancing emotional adjustment for military students by allowing them to associate with people who understand their experiences in ways that a nonveteran cannot. The SVO also assists in connecting members with local veterans services organizations so that they can gain support and mingle with veterans of diverse ages and generations. At SCSU, area Veterans of Foreign Wars posts and American Legion clubs support the SVO by providing funding and mentorship.

Another product of the SVO is advocacy, which increases awareness of the needs of veterans and helps to improve the campus environment for military students (see Chapter Eight). SVO advocates through panel discussions with university students, faculty, and staff. These panel discussions are held each semester during faculty and staff workshop days.

Summary

In order for colleges and universities to adequately address the needs of their student veteran population, effective resources in the form of financing, space, and equipment must be made available. Strong support from campus leadership and administration is vital in order for programs to facilitate college success for veterans, military members, and their families. Institutions of higher learning must identify veterans, provide access to resources and services, offer adequate gathering space for networking, and endeavor to integrate federal, state, and local resources. There is an urgent need for commitment and collaboration between academic affairs and student services, including clear role delineation and expectations, in order for cooperative programs between different entities to meet the needs of veterans.

The partnership between MDVA–Higher Education Veterans Programs and St. Cloud State University is an effective tool for meeting the needs of veterans. The MDVA–Higher Education Veterans Programs have been well received across Minnesota by higher education institutions, the military, service agencies, and the individuals being served. The program fills a gap in coordinated statewide postsecondary services for veterans, improving the experience for those who have found that starting and staying in college is often confusing and frustrating. Through coordinated programming, higher education institutions in Minnesota are ensuring that the current generation of veterans is provided the respect, appreciation, compassion, and services that they have earned and that they deserve.

References

Grieger, T. A., Cozza, S. J., Ursano, R. J., Hoge, C., Martinez, P. E., Engel, C. C., and Wain, H. J. "Posttraumatic Stress Disorder and Depression in Battle-Injured Soldiers." *American Journal of Psychiatry,* 2006, *163,* 1777–1783.

Hoge, C. W., Castro, C. A., Messer, S. C., McGurk, D., Cotting, D. I., and Koffman, R. L. "Combat Duty in Iraq and Afghanistan, Mental Health Problems, and Barriers to Care." *New England Journal of Medicine,* 2004, *351*(1), 13–22.

Lorge, E. M. "Army Responds to Rising Suicide Rates." *Army News Service.* [http://www.behavioralhealth.army.mil/news/20080131armyrespondstosuicide.html]. Jan. 31, 2008. Retrieved July 15, 2008.

Mills, D. "Army Taking Action to Stem Rising Suicide Rates." *U.S. Department of Defense American Forces Press Service News Articles.* [http://www.defenselink.mil/news/newsarticle.aspx?id=48834]. Jan. 31, 2008. Retrieved July 15, 2008.

Minnesota Office of Higher Education. "Minnesota GI Bill." [http://www.getreadyforcollege.org/gpg.cfm?pageid=1803]. 2007. Retrieved Dec. 26, 2008.

Minnesota State Colleges and Universities System. "Board of Trustees Policy 5.12." [http://www.mnscu.edu/board/policy/512.html]. 2007. Retrieved Dec. 26, 2008.

Minnesota State Colleges and Universities System. "Guard Online." [www.guardonline.mnscu.edu/]. 2008a. Retrieved Dec. 9, 2008.

Minnesota State Colleges and Universities System. "Veterans Services." [http://www.mnscu.edu/students/veterans/]. 2008b. Retrieved Jan. 3, 2009.

Pfeffer, D. S. "Report to the Minnesota National Guard, Minnesota Department of Veterans Affairs, and the Minnesota State Colleges and Universities system," 2007.

St. Cloud State University. "Veterans' Resources." [http://www.stcloudstate.edu/veterans/]. 2008. Retrieved Dec. 26, 2008.

State of Minnesota. "Higher Education Veterans Assistance Program (197.585)." [https://www.revisor.leg.state.mn.us/statutes/?id=197.585]. 2008a. Retrieved Dec. 26, 2008.

State of Minnesota. "Higher Education Fairness (197.775)." [https://www.revisor.leg.state.mn.us/statutes/?id=197.775&year=2008]. 2008b. Retrieved Dec. 26, 2008.

U.S. Department of Defense. "Task Force on Mental Health." [http://www.taps.org/%5Cdownload%5CDOD%20Mental%20Health%20Task%20Force%20Report.pdf]. 2007. Retrieved July 15, 2008.

Wisconsin Department of Veterans Affairs. "Report from Defense Manpower Data Center." [http://dva.state.wi.us/data/]. 2008. Retrieved July 15, 2008.

JAYNE M. LOKKEN is a psychologist in counseling and psychological services at St. Cloud State University and serves as advisor to the student veterans organization.

DONALD S. PFEFFER is veterans programs director at the Minnesota Department of Veterans Affairs–Higher Education Program. He served on active duty with the Air Force and in the Minnesota Air National Guard.

JAMES MCAULEY is a regional coordinator of veterans programs for the Minnesota Department of Veterans Affairs–Higher Education Program. He served on active duty with the Air Force and in the Air Force Reserve.

CHRISTOPHER STRONG is president of the student veterans organization and a history major at St. Cloud State University. He served on active duty in the Air Force.

New Directions for Student Services • DOI: 10.1002/ss

6

The lessons learned by campus personnel at Appalachian State University as they worked to meet the needs of student soldiers who were deployed during earlier conflicts provided a framework for programs and policies when students were deployed to Iraq and Afghanistan.

Ensuring the Success of Deploying Students: A Campus View

Teresa Johnson

Disruption of educational pursuits due to orders for military activation is inconvenient and discouraging to students who are soldiers. Deployment was an issue at institutions of higher education during Operations Desert Shield and Desert Storm in 1990 and 1991 and during the peace-keeping mission in Bosnia in 1996. Four weeks after the attacks of September 11, 2001, Operation Enduring Freedom began and student soldiers again faced the possibility that they would be deployed for active military duty. Operation Iraqi Freedom followed in March 2003. This chapter details the experiences at one higher education institution and the attempts there to assist students through the disruptions that resulted from deployments to active duty.

Appalachian State University has an enrollment of over 16,000, offers more than 140 undergraduate and graduate major programs, and is part of the University of North Carolina System. Located in the northwestern region of the state, Appalachian State is approximately four hours from Fort Bragg, Pope Air Force Base, and Seymour Johnson Air Force Base and six hours from Camp Lejeune. There are numerous National Guard and reserve units in close proximity to the campus.

Making the Transition from Student to Active-Duty Soldier

Beginning in 1990, students began withdrawing from Appalachian State University because of long-term military activations associated with Operation

NEW DIRECTIONS FOR STUDENT SERVICES, no. 126, Summer 2009 © Wiley Periodicals, Inc.
Published online in Wiley InterScience (www.interscience.wiley.com) • DOI: 10.1002/ss.316

Desert Shield and Operation Desert Storm. These students received orders to report to duty and had just a few days to take care of their personal affairs and address the interruption of their educational pursuits. It was an emotional time for them, for their families, and for the "Appalachian family" as well.

When students enlist in National Guard and reserve units, it is unlikely that they consider how their educational goals might be interrupted, particularly by a call to active duty and service in a war zone. A persuasive recruiter, feelings of patriotism, and GI Bill benefits are among the reasons to enlist. Typically, these units would be called upon to assist with natural disasters or crowd control in the United States. Students might expect that their duties will be limited to completing weekend drill each month and attending two weeks of training each year. However, the operational requirements of the military have changed. Student soldiers in the early 1990s realized that they would be called to active military duty and that there might be multiple deployments, possibly to a war zone overseas. Personnel at the university began to have a better understanding of these students' academic, financial, and emotional needs both before and after military activation. As a result, procedures were implemented to assist them.

When Operation Desert Shield began, administrative leaders at Appalachian State recognized the need to develop a plan for providing a smooth transition from student to soldier. The associate vice chancellor for student development, who was also the dean of students, and the veterans affairs coordinator initiated a meeting with the chief academic officer (the provost). The purpose of the meeting was to develop directives for how the institution would process students who received military orders that caused them to withdraw from the university. This effort was endorsed in advance by the chancellor of the university. Meeting with appropriate administrative staff and faculty, the associate vice chancellor for student development was able to secure support for an initiative that was designed to assist students who had to withdraw. The initiative was implemented near the end of the academic semester, in time for those who had been activated to take final exams early. The University of North Carolina General Administration also issued a system directive stating that students who were called to active military duty were entitled to a full refund of tuition and required fees. If they were recipients of other forms of financial aid, students were to meet with financial aid staff to determine the best course of action. If the student was not required to return federal, state, or institutional funds as a result of withdrawing, then a full refund of tuition and fees would be processed. If financial aid funds had to be returned and repayment would create a financial hardship, the student soldier would be advised not to withdraw. Students contacted their professors to make arrangements to receive incompletes or to complete coursework while off campus in order to receive course credit. Appalachian State followed the federal guidelines posted in the Federal Student Aid Handbook, Information for Financial Aid Professionals, in regard to withdrawal calculations (U.S. Department of Education, 2008).

NEW DIRECTIONS FOR STUDENT SERVICES • DOI: 10.1002/ss

As a result of the chancellor's support for deployed students, the provost and the Council of Chairs, a body consisting of all academic department chairpersons, notified faculty of the importance of working with students who were called to active military service and deployment. In response, professors developed creative options to allow students to complete courses if their deployment was close to the end of the semester. E-mail and Internet interaction between professors and students were the most popular options. In some instances, students were permitted to take their final exams before reporting to active duty, as long as they had completed all other coursework. Allowing students to complete the semester was an expression of the campus community's support for those individuals during a time of uncertainty and anxiety.

Once a withdrawal determination was made, the veterans affairs coordinator notified the U.S. Department of Veterans Affairs (VA) of the last date of attendance for students receiving GI Bill benefits or Dependent's Educational Assistance. Although the requirement to report punitive or nonpunitive grades was enforced, mitigating circumstances due to military activation were noted on the report to the VA. In 1996, another directive that was sent to Appalachian State University from the University of North Carolina General Administration stated that if students were involuntarily called to active duty in response to the peace-keeping mission in Bosnia, a full refund of tuition and required fees would be granted.

When the war on terrorism began in 2001, policies were already in place at Appalachian State to handle deployment-related student withdrawals. Moreover, because of the experience gained from the 1990s as a result of Desert Shield and Desert Storm, campus staff were prepared to assist students as they began the transition. As each student received deployment orders, a course of action that was in his or her best interest was determined, with assistance from the veterans affairs coordinator. For example, if deployment was during a period when the student was not enrolled, such as in the summer, he or she was directed to leave contact information with the associate vice chancellor for student development/dean of students and the veterans affairs coordinator. Establishing a connection with those administrators enabled the creation of a contact database that campus administrators used to answer students' questions about re-enrollment once the student soldier returned from active military duty; it was also a way to keep deployed students connected with the campus community. If deployment was during the semester, students were instructed to meet with their professors to work out a plan to withdraw, receive an incomplete grade, or finish a course via e-mail, parcel post mail, or the Internet. A precedent had been set during Desert Shield and Desert Storm and, therefore, faculty were willing to work with students and permit them to complete coursework if deployments occurred near the end of an academic term. In some instances, a professor determined that it would be in the best interest of the student to withdraw from the course. This decision was made in consultation with financial aid personnel. The registrar's office would process withdrawals based on the recommendations from financial aid staff and faculty. When students withdrew to report for active military duty, at least they understood their academic status and took comfort in knowing that they would be able to re-enroll upon their return from deployment. This assurance assisted in the transition from full-time student to full-time soldier, making it somewhat less stressful.

Continued Connection During Deployment

During Desert Shield and Desert Storm, the veterans affairs coordinator at Appalachian State established a process for maintaining contact with student soldiers who were deployed. Whether the deployed students were stateside or overseas, communications with them were consistent. Communications from Appalachian State included e-mails about campus happenings and copies of the university newspaper, *The Appalachian*. E-mail messages included practical, student-related information such as the process for early registration for classes when they returned and contact information for housing and residence life, financial aid, and other student services offices. T-shirts were mailed to deployed students to help them maintain their identification with the campus. Messages from campus leaders and students were shared with the soldiers, including pictures of supportive banners and signs posted on campus as well as photos of candlelight vigils and other events expressing support for the soldiers. Occasionally, a message of pleasant surprise would be sent, such as credits to student accounts for unused parking permits. Sharing this information with deployed students reminded them that they would be back on campus again and that Appalachian State University would be ready for their return.

In the early 1990s, student soldiers had left behind loved ones who had to cope with the emotional consequences of their deployment, so campus counseling and psychological staff had developed and maintained a Desert Shield Support Group, which met regularly on campus. This experience provided an excellent foundation on which to rebuild a support network in 2001. In addition, family support groups for dependents and friends of National Guard and reserve members were started. These groups planned and held holiday functions and other social events.

During fall 2004, the veterans affairs coordinator received information via e-mail from one of the soldiers that his National Guard unit might be released from active duty prior to the beginning of the spring 2005 semester. Several members of the unit wanted to enroll for the upcoming term. The veterans affairs coordinator immediately contacted the registrar to develop a process that would allow these soldiers to participate in early registration for the spring 2005 semester via the Internet. Each soldier had access to a curriculum planning sheet via the Appalachian State Web site and was able to select the appropriate courses for his or her major. Academic advising was also available to each soldier via e-mail. By November, many deployed soldiers had registered for classes for the 2005 spring semester but were still stationed in Iraq. According to policy, tuition and fees were due in December 2004, and nonpayment would result in cancellation of classes. The director of student accounts was able to suspend the policy and postpone payment until the beginning of the term for those soldiers. Provisions were made so that if the soldiers were unable to return to campus by the beginning of the upcoming term, the university would cancel their enrollment and no balance would be due for tuition and fees. However, if the soldiers were discharged in time for spring classes, they would already be registered and ready to make the transition back to student status. Extending the early registration option to students while they were deployed provided a meaningful link to the university and helped to ease the stress of deployment.

Transition from Military Duty to Student Life

When servicemembers returned to Appalachian State following the Gulf War, campus leaders were concerned about the adjustment to civilian and student life that they would need to make. The associate vice chancellor for student development/dean of students and the veterans affairs coordinator invited students who had been deployed to an informal gathering. The discussion that followed provided a healthy dialogue, and follow-up discussion sessions were planned. These exchanges provided university officials with the opportunity to evaluate the effectiveness of the policies and practices that had been put in place for student veterans.

Enhancing and Improving Support for
Student Veterans

Appalachian State University's efforts to implement processes for assisting students who were called to active military duty in the 1990s continued to be refined and improved when the war on terrorism began. A key component of the effort was the personal attention given to each student by faculty and staff members. This individualized approach proved to be an important contributing factor in facilitating a successful transition, whether the transition was from campus to active duty or from active duty to campus.

Another key to the success of the efforts at Appalachian State was the cooperation and collaboration of the administration and academic affairs. Because some members of the administrative and academic support network had been employed at the university for many years, they brought a sense of institutional history, an understanding of the campus culture, and commitment to student success. Moreover, they applied their professional expertise and problem-solving skills, enabling them to provide a high level of service to the unique student population represented by student soldiers.

NEW DIRECTIONS FOR STUDENT SERVICES • DOI: 10.1002/ss

Participation by university staff in professional organizations, such as the North Carolina Association of Coordinators of Veterans Affairs and the National Association of Veterans' Program Administrators, provides current information on changing policies and benefits in addition to networking opportunities. Maintaining contacts and working relationships with staff at education centers on military bases in the state, with county veterans services offices, the state division of veterans affairs, and the VA is also important.

Expanding and improving services for Appalachian State's student veterans continues to be a work in progress. Sometimes it just means doing the small and simple things; for example, university admissions literature now lists contact information for the veterans affairs coordinator. Beginning in the fall of 2008, an academic advisor for deploying students and veterans was designated. On the campus of Appalachian State University, the Veterans Memorial is a reminder of the sacrifice of members of the campus community, both past and present, who served their country and, in return, the commitment that university personnel and faculty have made to serve them.

Reference

U.S. Department of Education. "Federal Student Aid: Information for Financial Aid Professionals." [http://www.ifap.ed.gov/IFAPWebApp/index.jsp]. 2008. Retrieved Dec. 11, 2008.

Teresa Johnson is assistant director, Office of Student Financial Aid, at Appalachian State University, where she also serves as veterans affairs coordinator.

New Directions for Student Services • DOI: 10.1002/ss

This chapter describes how initiatives developed at the University of West Florida provide services for students who are on active duty around the world, as well as those stationed at bases in the region. Descriptions of programs and recommendations are also presented.

Connections, Partnerships, Opportunities, and Programs to Enhance Success for Military Students

Deborah Ford, Pamela Northrup, Lusharon Wiley

Active-duty personnel, reservists, veterans, and their spouses or dependents represent 30 percent of the 10,000 students at the University of West Florida (UWF). With base realignment activities, a rise in the number of troops returning from deployments, and an increase in military-affiliated students on campus, the needs of veterans and their families have become a top priority at UWF, as is the case at many colleges and universities.

Located in Pensacola, UWF is a regional comprehensive university in a community surrounded by military installations, including Pensacola Naval Air Station, Eglin Air Force Base, and Hurlburt Field. Administrators at the university, including those from student services and academic affairs, value partnerships with the military units in the region and work collaboratively with base leaders to provide learning opportunities for future generations of service personnel. UWF leaders place priority on developing programs and services to meet the diverse educational needs of students serving in the military. To fulfill this commitment, the university president appointed the ongoing President's Military Community Advisory Council, which comprises representatives from military installations in the area, retired officers, and key university personnel, including faculty. Academic programs serve as the anchor for the development and implementation of partnerships and opportunities to benefit military students at UWF. When

NEW DIRECTIONS FOR STUDENT SERVICES, no. 126, Summer 2009 © Wiley Periodicals, Inc.
Published online in Wiley InterScience (www.interscience.wiley.com) • DOI: 10.1002/ss.317

61

asked, these students emphasize that flexibility and convenience matter in the delivery of academic programs and support services.

The War Affects Campus Life at the University of West Florida

The world situation became very real to the UWF community in February 2003 when the president of the student government, along with other students, was called to service in Iraq. One day, he and his fellow students were majoring in business, education, or the humanities and participating in all aspects of campus life, and the next day they were in transit to a war zone. After serving a year in Iraq, they returned to a campuswide celebration in their honor, and to life as veterans of war. That former student government president has now completed his undergraduate and graduate degrees, is married, has served on the inaugural UWF Military Connections Committee, and was elected as the leader of the Pensacola Young Professionals Association. His leadership on campus, in the Army, and in the community exemplifies how veterans make a valuable contribution to student life. As leaders in higher education, our challenge is to create opportunities for continued success for our students, including active-duty military personnel, veterans, and reservists.

Military Personnel as Students in Higher Education

The total military-affiliated population in the United States represents a significant student recruitment source of college students, comprising approximately 2 million active-duty personnel, 25 million veterans, 411,000 reservists, and 659,000 Air Force and Army National Guard members (U.S. Department of Defense, 2008; U.S. Department of Veterans Affairs, 2008). The Department of Defense's off-duty voluntary education programs boast an enrollment of over 400,000 students annually in undergraduate and graduate courses. These numbers represent one of the largest for-credit continuing education operations in the world, accounting for approximately 19 percent of the total force eligible to participate in tuition assistance programs, and equaling $578 million in expenditures by the military for voluntary education (Baker, 2008). Baker also reported that 39,070 degrees were awarded to military personnel participating in voluntary education in the fiscal year 2006–07.

Meeting each servicemember's educational needs presents challenges at every level. Active-duty military personnel have significant pressures, including ongoing deployments and temporary duty assignments that often interfere with their availability to participate in voluntary education programs (see Chapters Two and Six). Because of the duties required of active-duty military personnel, postsecondary education typically can only be pursued part-time while off duty. Because these students may be deployed at any time, it is critical that university personnel make support services

NEW DIRECTIONS FOR STUDENT SERVICES • DOI: 10.1002/ss

accessible when students are available. Such efforts to make services accessible should include furnishing points of contact for support services both on military bases and on campus with hours of availability designed to facilitate contact for military personnel serving in worldwide time zones, as well as accommodating the need for flexibility in the types of learning opportunities available for military students.

National and Campus Organizations Facilitate Collaborations

Collaboration with national organizations also improves educational opportunities for military students at UWF. One organization, Servicemembers Opportunity Colleges (SOC), was established in 1972 in order to create and coordinate educational opportunities for servicemembers and their families. Partner schools accept transfer credit from other SOC members, maximizing access to higher education for students who are relocated or deployed. SOC is co-sponsored by the American Association of State Colleges and Universities and the American Association of Community Colleges, in partnership with other educational associations and the military services. Readers who are seeking to enhance educational opportunities for active-duty service personnel may want to consider contacting SOC in order to evaluate the benefits of participation for their own institution.

In addition, UWF personnel have made a commitment to learning as much as possible about military voluntary education through attending the conferences of the Florida Advisory Council on Military Education, the Council of College and Military Educators, and Department of Defense Worldwide, which is sponsored by Defense Activity for Non-Traditional Educational Support, an organization within the military that supports voluntary education. Connections with these organizations, as well as frequent and meaningful communication with military education offices, assist in shaping UWF's efforts to serve students and the military.

At the local level, the chief executive at UWF formed the President's Military Community Advisory Council in 2004 to enhance collaboration and communication with the military. The council, which includes retired military officers, military base leaders, faculty, deans, and administrators, meets quarterly to discuss initiatives under way at UWF and strives to make connections with the larger military community. The council also provides opportunities for collegial dialogue on major topics of shared interest to the university and the military. For example, UWF's participation in the congressionally supported Arabic Language and Culture certificate programs, designed for military personnel preparing to deploy to the Middle East, received much attention from the President's Community Military Advisory Council, which provided advice and made connections to aid successful implementation. Brigadier General Michael L. Ferguson, U.S. Army (Ret.), civilian aide to the Secretary of the Army, Florida (North), and member of the UWF President's Military Community Advisory Council, stated, "Those students with military experience and those associated in some manner with the military through families or ROTC, invariably constitute a most valued constituency because of their maturity, desire to excel, and character. Often academic institutions fail to partner with these students and their services and tap their invaluable ideas, experience, and resources. UWF has recognized that the military, above almost all institutions, stresses growth in leadership and productivity through higher education" (Michael L. Ferguson, personal communication, July 25, 2008).

Academic Programs That Enhance the Success of Military Students

Nationally, students are selecting distance learning courses at a higher rate than ever before. At higher education institutions in the United States, more than 3.5 million students are taking at least one distance learning course per semester, accounting for approximately 20 percent of all students (Allen and Seaman, 2007). For active-duty military students, the enrollment rate for distance learning courses is even greater. In 2007, the Navy reported a total of 43,071 personnel taking distance learning courses, 19,321 taking courses on base, and 11,274 off base. Approximately 18 percent of all active-duty Navy personnel participated in off-duty educational opportunities (Hunter, 2008). The Air Force reported that in 2003, of the personnel who were taking courses, 24 percent chose distance learning. By 2006, this figure had increased to 44 percent (Smith, 2007).

Internet-based distance courses account for significant enrollment numbers; however, there are still approximately 150,000 deployed service personnel who have limited access to the Internet. Using funding from two Department of Defense congressional budget appropriations, the U.S. Navy and UWF are collaborating to test mobile devices as a means to provide access to education when access to the Internet is limited or unavailable. UWF's Academic Technology Center developed a series of programs that are offered as complete for-credit courses and available on mobile devices such as personal digital assistants (PDAs) and ultra-portable devices. Service personnel who are deployed or preparing to deploy can take these devices with them and work in an individualized mode of instruction while on the go. When access is available, the student will connect to the Internet and communicate with the instructor via Web conferencing on the ultra-portable device. This technology opens the door for service personnel who otherwise would have to delay their education while deployed. These mobile models of learning continue to be tested by soldiers and sailors throughout the world, including combat zones.

In addition to meeting the diverse needs of active-duty personnel, veterans, and families through online learning, UWF has partnered with local entities, including Workforce Escarosa, the Workforce Development Board

NEW DIRECTIONS FOR STUDENT SERVICES • DOI: 10.1002/ss

of Okaloosa and Walton Counties in Florida, and school districts in local counties, to create Hometown Heroes Teach (University of West Florida, 2008a). This program meets two important needs in the region: it prepares eligible wounded and disabled veterans for careers in teaching while providing quality teachers in a region facing a critical shortage.

Student Services and Support Programs to Assist Military Learners

In 2006, UWF answered the call from the National Association of Student Personnel Administrators to be more intentional in developing programs and services to support military personnel, veterans, and their families. The chief student affairs officer at UWF, in response to the growing needs of veterans and their families, formed the Military Connections Committee. Members of this committee, chaired by the associate dean of students, include retired veterans, ROTC members, community members, the campus veterans affairs representative, and faculty. The mission of the Military Connections Committee is to serve as a resource network and information center for student military personnel and their families. The committee advocates for inclusive policies that address military concerns and sponsors activities that recognize military personnel and their contributions. The committee also developed a checklist for students affiliated with the military, created an informational packet for returning veterans, established a support group, conducted a needs assessment to improve services for students in the military, sponsored an annual Military Appreciation Day, and adopted the slogan "UWF cares about veterans." Ultimately, the Military Connections Committee hopes to expand its role in order to work with other campus departments to develop transitional strategies that will allow veterans to successfully navigate the bureaucracy associated with attending an institution of higher learning.

As part of the effort to enhance campus communication for military students, the University of West Florida's Veterans Services Office established an online newsletter for veterans (University of West Florida, 2008b). A Web site, maintained by the staff of the Veterans Services Office, provides students with up-to-date information on registration, U.S. Department of Veterans Affairs (VA) certification, and other frequently asked questions.

Perhaps the greatest need of many returning veterans is assistance in addressing psychological and social problems associated with post-traumatic stress disorder (PTSD), traumatic brain injury, or multiple physical injuries. Each of these is emerging as a significant area of concern for combat veterans (see Chapters Four and Nine), as is their occurrence in combination. Sachs (2008) cautions that educational achievement can be complicated because "in addition to specific disorders such as traumatic brain injury and post-traumatic stress disorder, combat veterans experience psychosocial disruption as they rapidly transition from the role of warrior to that of student" (p. 1).

The Student Disability Resource Center (SDRC) at UWF has seen an increase in veterans who have either multiple injuries or a combination of PTSD and unresolved anger applying for services. A complicating factor for some veterans seems to be relationship building with other students. In fact, in response to an SDRC survey, one student wrote, "It might be nice if someone wanted to share a story about their transition from military to school to work." This statement reinforces the idea that returning veterans need support and understanding from the campus community.

Not only are veterans feeling the pressure of entering an academic environment that they may not have experienced before, but many of them are also dealing with the impact of injuries. To address these concerns, the Military Connections Committee, the Veterans Services Office, Vocational Rehabilitation, the Counseling Center, and the SDRC are working together to establish best practices for responding to these increasing demands. In addition to the online newsletter, the University of West Florida is collaborating with the local VA office to place a counselor on site at the university.

In addition, the Military Connections Committee is working with student veterans to establish a Student Veterans of America group on campus (see Chapter Eight). The Military Connections Committee continues to refine UWF's approach to providing services to its military students. Students with military experience were surveyed in 2006 and again in 2008. The purpose of the biannual surveys was to assess the effectiveness of support services delivery, to identify areas for improvement, and to solicit suggestions. A number of concerns were expressed by participants in the 2008 survey, including issues pertaining to course offerings, tuition deferments, and problems encountered by students when they transfer out of the area. Survey comments singled out course offerings as a particular concern because they were not tailored to adult learners, the courses are often offered at inconvenient times for working adults, they are not offered frequently enough, and there are a limited number of online offerings. University administrators are addressing these concerns by encouraging collaboration across departments on campus, building community support, reviewing policies, and continuing to educate faculty and staff on the needs of military students.

Recommendations on How to Enhance the Success of Military Students

Creating connections, partnerships, and opportunities to enhance the educational success of military learners is a challenge for any college or university. Following are some recommendations for campus professionals who are interested in developing new partnerships or enhancing existing programs for military students and their families:

New Directions for Student Services • DOI: 10.1002/ss

- Consider appointing a group of faculty, staff, and students to study the needs of military students and veterans and to make recommendations to improve the quality of programs and services. Establishing such a group is most effective when it is undertaken as an initiative of a senior administrator, preferably the president.
- Learn about professional associations and networks affiliated with military education, including the Council of Colleges and Military Educators (ccmeonline.org), the Advisory Council on Military Education (www.fla-acme.org or ccmeonline.org for state specific information), the Servicemembers Opportunity College (www.soc.aascu.org), and Defense Activity for Non-Traditional Educational Support (www.dantes.doded.mil).
- Determine whether the student information system on your campus collects specific demographic information about military students. If not, work with the appropriate administrator to add data fields for military students, veterans, and their spouses and dependents. Identifying military students is critical to communicating effectively with them!
- Conduct a survey and host conversations to understand the needs of military students on campus. Topics and questions might include the following: As a veteran and student, what is your greatest issue or concern on campus? What services would you like to see posted on the campus Web site for veterans? Do you know the location of the Web site for the campus veterans affairs office? Have you used the site? Would you be interested in joining a student veterans organization on campus? What news items would you like to see in a newsletter for military students?
- Develop seamless enrollment and transition processes for reaching out to prospective and current students who are in the military. Outreach efforts should be extended to the families of military students. Such outreach efforts might include Web sites, newsletters, enrollment personnel, or counseling professionals dedicated to serving these students.
- Create flexible academic programs and support services to meet the demanding schedules of military students.
- Engage with military leaders, including retired personnel, to develop programs and services that meet the needs of active-duty students. Elizabeth O'Herrin, former Student Veterans of America (SVA) executive director, stated, "Currently, most institutions of higher education are not providing student-veterans the resources they need to succeed. That's where SVA goes to work: peer to peer support is the key to helping veterans attain success in higher education and SVA is dedicated to providing resources on campus to provide veterans the tools they need in order to get the education they deserve" (Lanigan, 2008, p. 14). Along these lines, the chief student affairs officer could appoint a task force of military students and student life personnel to collaborate with local Veterans of Foreign Wars (VFW) posts to create an SVA chapter on campus. According to Lanigan (2008), there were fifty-four SVA chapters in September 2008, and the organization plans to expand. It is helpful to note that national

veterans groups such as the VFW have been instrumental in the development and support of SVA chapters.

- Create programs to show appreciation for military service to the country. Examples include annual appreciation programs and campuswide events on Memorial Day, September 11, and Veterans Day.
- Lead a campuswide effort to lobby state and federal officials for funding for campus programs to meet the unique needs of military students. Empower faculty, staff, and students to serve as informed voices in support of lobbying efforts.
- Take the lead to coordinate services among campus units, including academic affairs, veterans affairs, financial aid, counseling, student disability services, academic support services, and others, in order to provide seamless enrollment and transitional services for military students. *Learning Reconsidered,* the influential work that calls for a campuswide focus on student learning (Keeling, 2004), suggests that student affairs educators need to take a leading role in such endeavors.

Conclusion

As you review the recommendations in this chapter, consider how receptive your campus will be to enhancing the delivery of academic programs, to improving support services, and to increasing understanding in order to meet the needs of military students. Through connections, partnerships, opportunities, and programs, the needs of military college students today and in the future can be met. It is the responsibility of campus leaders, including those in student affairs, to first act locally and then partner with military leaders to meet the unique needs of the increasing population of students who are in the military. Without the determined leadership of student affairs officers, it is unlikely that campus efforts will be as successful as they need to be to help repay these students for their service.

References

Allen, E., and Seaman, J. "Online Nation: Five Years of Growth in Online Education." [www.sloan-c.org/publications/survey/index.asp]. 2007. Retrieved Feb. 12, 2008.

Baker, C. "Voluntary Education Briefing." Presented at the annual meeting of the Florida Advisory Council on Military Education, Jacksonville. [www.voled.doded.mil/voled_Web/library/slides/voled_overview.pdf]. April 21–23, 2008. Retrieved May 1, 2008.

Hunter, A. "Navy Voluntary Education." Presented at the annual meeting of the Council of College and Military Educators, San Francisco. [www.ccmeonline.org]. February 18–21, 2008. Retrieved May 15, 2008.

Keeling, R. (ed.). *Learning Reconsidered: A Campus-Wide Focus on the Student Experience.* Washington, D.C.: National Association of Student Personnel Administrators and American College Personnel Association, 2004.

Lanigan, K. "Vets Clubs Offer Peer Support on Campus." *VFW Magazine,* 2008, *96*(1), 14–19.

Sachs, R. "Valuing Veterans." [http://www.insidehighered.com/views/2008/06/12/c2c]. 2008. Retrieved Dec. 14, 2008.

Smith, A. M. "Air Force Voluntary Education Update." Presented at the annual meeting of Council of College and Military Educators, Monterey, Calif. [www.ccmeonline.org/overview.asp?yr=2007]. January 22–25, 2007. Retrieved Oct. 14, 2008.

University of West Florida. "Hometown Heroes Teach." [http://www.uwf.edu/hometownheroesteach/]. 2008a. Retrieved Dec. 9, 2008.

University of West Florida. "Veterans Services Office Newsletter." [https://nautical.uwf.edu/files/module/groupMail/200809_VA_Newsletter_1.docx]. 2008b. Retrieved Dec. 9, 2008.

U.S. Department of Defense. "Military Personnel Statistics." [http://siadapp.dmdc.osd.mil/personnel/MILITARY/Miltop.htm]. 2008. Retrieved May 1, 2008.

U.S. Department of Veterans Affairs. "About VA Home." [www.va.gov/about_va/]. 2008. Retrieved June 16, 2008.

DEBORAH FORD is vice president for student affairs at the University of West Florida.

PAMELA NORTHRUP is associate provost at the University of West Florida.

LUSHARON WILEY is assistant dean of students for leadership programs and the student disability resource center at the University of West Florida.

8

Involvement in campus organizations can be an important factor in student success. Student veterans organizations are becoming common on college campuses as students who have served in the military seek the sense of community that comes from joining with other veterans in shared purpose.

Student Veterans Organizations

John Summerlot, Sean-Michael Green, Daniel Parker

Following World War II, when the United States faced both the challenge of demilitarization of millions of service personnel and the end of the wartime economy, the linking of military service and educational benefits was introduced into the American ethos. Benefits in the form of the GI Bill led millions of veterans to college, and they arrived with a different set of experiences, goals, and interests than did nonveteran students. The idea that college-going veterans were different from civilian students led to the development of programs and offices staffed with persons who offered assistance with tasks such as completing GI Bill paperwork and exploring career aspirations. On many campuses, students who were veterans formed organizations designed to meet their own unique needs. Some of these organizations affiliated with other groups such as the American Veterans Committee (Saxe, 2007), but many were homegrown groups focused on local issues such as housing shortages and the transition to college life. Student organizations for veterans remained in place on many campuses and provided support for veterans of the Korean War. As the World War II and Korean War veterans graduated and moved on, these offices and organizations slowly began to diminish in size and staffing, reflecting the decline in the number of students who were veterans.

Veterans of the Vietnam conflict faced different challenges. As that war effort lost popular support, veterans of the conflict, including those on college campuses, became the targets of protest (DeBenedetti, 1990). For the first time, many college students found themselves better off not identifying as veterans, so they attempted to blend in with their fellow students as much as possible. Some college and university campuses experienced an

NEW DIRECTIONS FOR STUDENT SERVICES, no. 126, Summer 2009   © Wiley Periodicals, Inc.
Published online in Wiley InterScience (www.interscience.wiley.com) • DOI: 10.1002/ss.318

increase in anti-military or anti-war groups. These groups tried to remove Reserve Officers' Training Corps (ROTC) programs and held rallies to end the war. Some veterans became involved in the anti-war movement as well, often through campus chapters such as Vietnam Veterans Against the War (Hunt, 1999).

The post-Vietnam Cold War period offered less controversy, and veterans who were students encountered a postsecondary system characterized by indifference to the military. Campus administrators and the programs they offered in support of veterans were once again reduced in number and scope as the presence of veterans on campuses declined. Although numbers from earlier wars are dwindling, people representing each of these time periods, particularly Vietnam and post-Vietnam eras, are present on campuses today. Senior faculty and administrators may hold beliefs and views that they developed as students during the era of anti-war protests in the 1960s and 1970s. Mid-level administrators and faculty may have come of age in the ambivalent 1980s. There are entry-level administrators and faculty whose initial experience with a nation at war was the first Gulf War. And some of the current students and staff, too young to remember the first Gulf War, know only the post–September 11 perspective and the attitudes of society toward the wars in Iraq and Afghanistan.

Military conflicts and the stories of those sent to fight them are becoming an important part of contemporary social culture (Carroll, 2006). Once again, student veterans are becoming an increasingly large subgroup of the college student population. Students who have experienced conflict as members of the military come to college expecting to be supported, if not honored for their service. One way that campus administrators can facilitate transitions for student veterans is to assist in founding and maintaining campus-based student organizations for veterans. Military service is a bonding experience because individual safety and security often depends on cohesive group efforts. Student veterans, once they are on campus, will look to replace the cohesion of their unit by seeking out others who have had similar experiences. An active student organization for veterans can become this point of connection for student veterans who are new to campus. The goals of a student veteran organization should include aiding veterans with the adjustment to campus life and using group influence to advocate for changes that will help student veterans achieve their academic goals. This chapter details factors to be considered by those who are committed to assisting students who are making a transition from combat to campus.

Campus Climate

Hurtado, Milem, Clayton-Pederson, and Allen (1999) describe campus climate as a set of "current perceptions, attitudes, and expectations that define the institution and its members" (p. 2). The climate that veterans experience on campus is determined at multiple levels, and an understanding of the climate is helpful in framing a discussion of student veteran organizations. Many factors influence campus climate, including policies; practices; attitudes of faculty, staff, and students; and the local community itself.

The contributors to this chapter are veterans who, upon return to civilian life and college, joined campus-based student veterans organizations. Here we share our collective experiences, gained from several college campuses and from conversations with student veterans from around the country. As a result of our conversations, we have identified three types of campus climates that explain how students who are also veterans can expect to experience their campus community: supportive, ambivalent, and challenging.

Supportive Climate. When students who are veterans speak of veteran-friendly campuses, they are referring to campuses where institutionally based efforts are made to support veterans. Supportive campus climates are most likely found at colleges and universities that have strong historic ties to the military. Often, they are land-grant institutions, are located near a military base, or have a long history of successful and vibrant ROTC programs. This type of campus will likely have a veterans affairs office with adequate staffing, an active student veterans organization (SVO), and policies in place that reflect the needs of veterans.

In a supportive environment, veterans are unlikely to feel the need to hide their military affiliation. Many of these supportive campuses are veteran-friendly and strive to supply infrastructure to support veterans— for example, pre-college programs or specialized enrollment counselors. At supportive campuses, veterans may be serving as administrators and faculty in an atmosphere where community members are readily identified as being former military members.

Ambivalent Climate. An ambivalent climate is most likely found at urban or commuter campuses, institutions with large numbers of nontraditional students. In the ambivalent environment, military service is viewed as just another pre-college experience. Veterans who are students can blend in with ease in an environment of nontraditional students and commuters, but they may have a more difficult time connecting with their veteran peers. These institutions are often in settings where veterans feel less connected to the campus and may seek involvement with off-campus veterans groups. In this environment, veterans receive little recognition, if any, and minimal campus-based support services.

Challenging Climate. A challenging climate is usually found at schools with a history of political dissent and strong anti-military movements. These types of institutions (or subgroups such as individual colleges or programs within a university) have climates that challenge any links between the campus community and the military. Veterans at these schools often do not identify themselves as veterans due to the fact that reactions to military service can be varied and emotionally charged; instead, they opt to conceal their military experience. Concealment allows them the freedom to speak their mind without being judged for being a veteran and protects them from becoming

NEW DIRECTIONS FOR STUDENT SERVICES • DOI: 10.1002/ss

targets of criticism from those on campus who hold anti-military views. This concealment often extends to the classroom.

In each of these climates—supportive, ambivalent, and challenging—it may be difficult for veterans to interact with some members of the faculty. For a veteran who has become accustomed to strict organizational discipline and high accountability, the laissez-faire culture of the academy may be frustrating. In the military, the chain of command clarifies who has authority, but it is not always clear who is in charge on campus. If a faculty member demonstrates lack of respect for institutional authority and policies, veterans, trained under a different philosophy, may view such criticism as disloyalty. Also, open criticism of military service and the government in the classroom may cause military-affiliated students to feel threatened or unwelcome.

Why Are Student Veterans Organizations Important?

The role that student veterans organizations are playing on campuses is similar to that of other organizations that are formed to pursue the interests of unique student populations. Veterans are interested in connecting with fellow students who have similar experiences. Student organizations provide a vehicle through which veterans can express a collective voice of advocacy while also supplying a setting for learning, reflection, and participation beyond the traditional classroom. It is important to note that a student veterans organization can provide an environment to support transition from the military to the campus.

An SVO provides student veterans with a relatively risk-free atmosphere in which to interact with peers who are familiar with the language and culture of the military. An SVO can also afford its members a safe harbor away from the probing questions that sometimes arise in interactions with students who have no military experience (see Chapter One). Student veteran organizations can function as social clubs, orientation groups, and information exchanges. SVOs may also serve as political action groups and transition aids, supplying links to the campus community like those that other student organizations provide for their members.

In a challenging climate, an SVO provides opportunities for veterans to display their military identity, free of judgment from others. On the Indiana University campus, the IU Vet Club's biweekly social events are occasions for members to escape the constraints of a challenging campus climate and relax in a zone that is safe from criticism. Club members use their time together not to relive their combat experiences but to share strategies for coping with campus life, with difficult courses, with family concerns, and with the issues of transition to college and life as civilians.

Veterans in ambivalent climates may use student veterans organizations for the purposes of networking and peer mentoring. The University of Pittsburgh, for example, attracts many nontraditional and commuter students. Student veterans use their SVO membership to forge professional, academic, and social bonds with their peers. Much of the support and discussion is not specific talk about the veteran status of members but general conversation about career and family. For many, membership in the veterans club provides their most meaningful out-of-class connection with the campus.

In supportive climates, club members often provide campus personnel with ideas about how to better serve and support veterans. Club members identify the needs of student veterans and work with others across the campus, including student services personnel, to meet those needs. And SVOs serve as an important starting point for student veterans who are new to a campus, helping them to find information about support services and opportunities.

How Are Student Veterans Organizations Formed?

Most commonly, the idea of starting an SVO originates with student veterans themselves, typically in response to the need to identify with others on campus and work together to enhance the academic success of veterans. There are also cases in which administrators and others on campus see a need and facilitate formation of an SVO. For instance, in the same year at the University of Pittsburgh, two SVOs emerged: one supported by an administrator and another by a faculty member, both of whom were veterans.

However, not all SVOs are formed in a purposeful and intentional manner. The original gathering of veterans at the University of Kansas (KU), for example, took place not with the intent of creating a stronger veterans community but for a photo shoot for the Veterans of Foreign Wars magazine in the summer of 2006. During the photo shoot, a few of the student veterans began to discuss the challenges of being a veteran at KU. Through their individual experiences, they realized that the campus did not have the resources to serve their needs. That evening, they catalogued their concerns about the university's bureaucracy and how, as veterans, they were underserved. KU had grouped the student veterans with other nontraditional students who were married or had children and assumed that their needs were being met. It took the chance meeting of a significant number of the campus veterans to see a need for action as a group. As a result, an SVO was formed at KU and remains active.

Regardless of how they are started, student veterans organizations have the potential to support veterans by providing points of connection to the campus and by using the strength of the peer group to give voice to the needs and interests of a unique population of students.

How Are Student Veterans Organizations Structured?

Student veterans organizations are generally dependent on student leadership but likely must also rely on an advisor. If an institution has a professional staff member who is responsible for veteran's services, that individual may be the advisor. More often, there is no interested professional staff member with those responsibilities or the SVO pre-dates such a position. In these cases, it is not uncommon for a veteran from the campus who is a faculty member or administrator to serve as the advisor. An advisor serves several functions— for example, providing the SVO with a connection to the larger campus community. This duty can include providing feedback to staff members who serve veterans, such as the official who certifies veterans benefits. Clearly, there are distinctions between the roles of the SVO advisor and the campus personnel responsible for providing services to students; coordinating their efforts is generally useful.

This section provides several examples of the ways that faculty, staff, and administrators on a campus can be involved with a student veterans organization. Given the mix of policies and practices, it is probably best left to the students to determine the structure and purpose of their own organization, including how membership is defined and the role of the advisor.

The certifying official for campus transactions of interest to the U.S. Department of Veterans Affairs (VA) can be a source of advocacy for the SVO. However, many certifying officials are financial aid personnel, often clerical or support staff, who have seen their duties increase as the population of veterans grows. On a moderately sized campus, mandatory reports for the VA, including veterans' certifications, provide more than enough work and may limit opportunities for the certifying official to expand his or her role to advocate on behalf of student veterans, even on campus issues. While campus staffing levels vary widely, it is important to have a veterans services officer as the key person in assisting this emerging population of students because he or she represents the school's central administration.

Marketing SVOs to potential members can occur through the same avenues that are open to other student groups. Providing information at student life activities, posting on campus bulletin boards, and attending informational sessions can be effective. In addition, some SVOs use the VA certifying official to help promote the organization. As an SVO was forming at the University of Pittsburgh, the university administrator associated with the group contacted the Office of Veteran Affairs on campus to obtain the campus e-mail addresses for all veterans who were registered for military benefits, thus acquiring an initial database of potential members.

Depending on campus resources, SVOs may have designated office or club space. Some institutions make a common office space available for student organizations, an area the SVO should use, if only to connect with other members of student interest groups. Sometimes the office of the professional or clerical staff member who serves the campus veterans community will serve as a meeting place and work space for the members. At Mississippi State University, the Sonny Montgomery Center for America's Veterans serves as a cultural center for veterans, houses the clerical and professional support staff, and provides common meeting and social space for veterans to use between classes.

A common difference between formal and informal groups is recognition by the institution. At Indiana University, the University of Kansas, Mississippi State University, the University of Nevada, Las Vegas, and on other campuses, SVOs have obtained formal recognition, have access to meeting rooms, and can request funding from the student government. On the other hand, the informal SVO at the University of Pittsburgh, although it continues to meet, has not applied for recognition.

What Do Student Veterans Organizations Do?

Student veterans organizations can serve students in a variety of ways including advocacy. For example, among the early issues that the University of Kansas SVO dealt with were delayed benefits payments from the federal government to the university. The institution was not taking into consideration that GI Bill benefits are paid out on a monthly basis rather than at the start of the semester as are other scholarships. This situation caused many financial challenges for veterans, who were required to pay tuition and fees up front in a lump sum. Part of the collective effort by the SVO members was a proposal that veterans be permitted to pay for their books in monthly installments over the course of the semester. The student veterans worked closely with administrators and KU bookstore personnel to develop interest-free payment programs for both books and tuition. These reforms were accomplished through a series of meetings attended by the representatives from the KU Collegiate Veterans Association, the registrar and bursar's offices, and the bookstores (University of Kansas Collegiate Veterans Association, 2008).

On many campuses, student veterans groups have also been influential in persuading administrators to adopt withdrawal and re-enrollment policies that protect students who are called to service through the reserves or National Guard. These policies can affect students in many areas, including housing, financial aid, and GI Bill benefits payments. Veterans who are deployed for twelve to eighteen months may also be challenged by having to reapply for admission to the university unless policies are put in place to facilitate and support their return to campus (see Chapter Six). The SVO can monitor the extent to which policies affecting veterans are, in fact, veteran-friendly.

SVOs sponsor a variety of formal and informal activities, reflecting the interests of their members and the needs of the campus. An example of one of the more formal types of activities is a mentoring program established by the SVO at Indiana University. New students who are veterans can choose to have a mentor, selected from SVO upper-division volunteers or from faculty and administrators who are veterans. The program is intended to serve at least two functions: (1) to give the new student veteran direct support for his or her transition and (2) to provide an early warning system in which a veterans services official on campus is alerted if the transition does not appear to be going well.

Student veterans organizations, particularly during their formative period, may not have planned events. For example, a veterans group began at the University of Pittsburgh with a simple informational meeting. The interest group met five additional times over the next two semesters; each meeting had an open agenda. Goals were discussed without achieving consensus, and no budget was formulated. Rather, the participating students seemed content to leave the group as an informal network and gathering of peers.

Some student veterans groups have become active at the state level by lobbying on issues of concern. For instance, the student veterans in Kansas worked to get the state legislature to recognize the growing gap between the cost of higher education and the amount that the GI Bill paid. The KU SVO proposed legislation that would have covered the costs of tuition for veterans, leaving GI Bill money for living expenses. While this legislation did not pass, members of the SVO gained valuable experience and were able to secure a limited number of state-funded scholarships for veterans.

As SVOs become active on campuses, opportunities for involvement will likely present themselves, sometimes in unanticipated ways. In the spring of 2008, an administrator at Indiana University who also was a veteran approached the SVO membership about ways that the university could help nonveterans understand why veterans are a student population with special needs. After some discussion, it was decided to propose a course on the connections between veterans and higher education. The course was approved for two credits through the School of Education, and student veterans then helped get the word out about the course. Some veterans enrolled for the course, along with a number of nonveterans.

In the spring of 2007, a national organization, Student Veterans of American (SVA), began as a grassroots effort to mobilize student veterans from different campuses on the issue of education benefits at both state and national levels. SVA, consisting of campus student veterans organizations, elected leaders from among member SVOs. The SVA encouraged its members to become politically involved by lobbying in support of the Post-9/11 GI Bill (see Chapter Ten). The leadership of the Student Veterans of America met in Washington, D.C., with congressional leaders to advocate for federal funding for student veterans programs, an effort that will likely continue for the foreseeable future.

Concluding Thoughts

While student veterans organizations vary in scope, focus, and structure, they also have common traits. SVOs are typically egalitarian organizations, without regard to rank, branch of service, or time in service. SVOs also provide support services and programs designed to orient student veterans to campus and assist in their reacclimation to civilian life. SVOs function as advocates for issues that are important to student veterans, providing a means for these students to support one another. Student groups can work informally outside the bureaucratic structures that exist at institutions of higher learning, particularly by finding ways to link administrative units as advocates for improvements in services. The SVO can be an invaluable tool for guiding an institution in how to meet the needs of current and future student veterans. Perhaps most important, the fellowship and support provided by an SVO facilitates the transition that students are making from one lifestyle to another by offering a means for connection and reflection, always for the purpose of helping students to achieve their academic and developmental objectives.

References

Carroll, A. (ed.). *Operation Homecoming: Iraq, Afghanistan, and the Home Front, in the Words of the U.S. Troops and Their Families.* New York: Random House, 2006.

DeBenedetti, C. *An American Ordeal: The Antiwar Movement of the Vietnam War.* Syracuse, N.Y.: Syracuse University Press, 1990.

Hunt, A. E. *The Turning: A History of Vietnam Veterans Against the War.* New York: New York University Press, 1999.

Hurtado, S., Milem, J., Clayton-Pederson, A., and Allen, W. *Enhancing Diverse Learning Environments: Improving the Climate for Racial/Ethnic Diversity in Higher Education.* Washington, D.C.: George Washington University, 1999. (ED 430 513)

Saxe, R. F. *Settling Down: World War II Veterans' Challenge to the Postwar Consensus.* New York: Palgrave Macmillan, 2007.

University of Kansas Collegiate Veterans Association. "KU Collegiate Veterans Home." [www.kuveterans.org]. 2008. Retrieved Dec. 17, 2008.

JOHN SUMMERLOT *is a residence manager at Indiana University Bloomington, where he is also pursuing his doctorate. He served as a Marine before college and with the Army National Guard during college.*

SEAN-MICHAEL GREEN *is associate dean in the Division of Graduate and Continuing Education at Westfield State College. He served on active duty as a Marine.*

DANIEL PARKER *is completing a B.A. in political science at the University of Kansas. He is a former Marine sergeant who served two tours in Iraq and founded the University of Kansas Collegiate Veterans Association.*

9

Severely injured military veterans of the conflicts in Iraq and Afghanistan who are completing rehabilitation at a military hospital and are ready to pursue postsecondary instruction are assisted by an academic advisor at the hospital and a mentor from a cooperating college or university.

Partnering to Assist Disabled Veterans in Transition

David DiRamio, Michele Spires

In his final public speech, delivered in 1977, Hubert H. Humphrey famously quipped that the moral test of our nation includes how we care for "those who are in the shadows of life: the sick, the needy, and the handicapped" (Cohen, 1978, p. 491). Today, America is being put to that test, for it is being challenged to meet the needs of unprecedented numbers of wounded and disabled veterans returning from military service. In past conflicts such as those in Korea and Vietnam, approximately three servicemembers were wounded for every one who died. However, in the current conflict in Iraq, the ratio of wounded—including combat-related and noncombat-related injuries—to dead is closer to sixteen to one (Stiglitz and Bilmes, 2008). Undoubtedly, an increasing number of disabled veterans will be seeking postsecondary education in the next few years. Are college and university personnel ready to meet the needs of this unique student population?

This chapter is designed to inform the reader about students who are disabled veterans, and it describes one initiative to support the success of those who are severely injured. While many of the wounded suffer from traditional war injuries to bone and muscle, an expanded list of service-related disabilities includes traumatic brain injury (TBI) and post-traumatic stress disorder (PTSD). It is important that campus personnel, including faculty members, understand that many veterans have more than one difficulty

The authors thank James Selbe, assistant vice president for program evaluations at the American Council on Education, for his assistance in the preparation of this chapter.

NEW DIRECTIONS FOR STUDENT SERVICES, no. 126, Summer 2009 © Wiley Periodicals, Inc.
Published online in Wiley InterScience (www.interscience.wiley.com) • DOI: 10.1002/ss.319

that affects their learning and may have multiple disability diagnoses. When servicemembers with these types of injuries return to civilian life, they face tough transitions and often lose the convenience of direct access to the government's educational support programs. Past direct support likely included conveniences such as an education service officer overseeing the voluntary education programs and academic programs or classes offered on base. Perhaps postsecondary institutions can lead the nation as exemplars for working with disabled veterans and ensuring their success in the academic enterprise. This effort can make education the catalyst for a rewarding reintegration into civilian life. This is a tall order and perhaps beyond the scope of higher education's mission, but in this era of accountability, colleges and universities are uniquely positioned to provide services for disabled veterans seeking postsecondary instruction.

Between March 2003 and September 2008, more than 30,634 service personnel were injured during Operation Iraqi Freedom (iCasualties.org, 2008), and bone and muscle injuries accounted for more than 40 percent of the total (Ephron, 2007). The most common of these injuries occurred to soft tissue or bone and typically resulted from an improvised explosive device (IED) blast or gunshot wound. A majority of the wounded receive treatment and return to their unit. However, the most severely wounded undergo multiple surgeries and likely spend many months rehabilitating at military hospitals such as Walter Reed Army Medical Center.

Estimates are that between 11 and 28 percent of combat troops suffer some level of traumatic brain injury (TBI), a condition often arising from exposure to the concussive blast of an IED or other explosion (Zoroya, 2007). TBI is becoming known as the signature injury of this generation of war fighters (Emmons, 2006). Diagnosis of TBI is difficult because symptoms may not reveal themselves until many months after the initial trauma. This type of brain injury will affect a veteran cognitively, physically, behaviorally, or in a combination of those ways. Cognitive problems include inability to concentrate and loss of memory. Headaches, dizziness, and blurred vision are some of the physical symptoms of TBI. Often discovered along with other medical problems, TBI-related behavioral changes include irritability, anxiety, sleep disorders, and depression.

Referred to in past wars as *shell shock* or *combat fatigue,* post-traumatic stress disorder, Kinchin (2005) suggested, is an invisible injury and is essentially a normal human reaction to an abnormal and traumatic event. Characterized as an anxiety disorder, PTSD produces symptoms such as intrusive thoughts about a traumatic event, avoiding stimuli that remind the person of the event, emotional numbness, and physiological hyper-arousal. According to the U.S. Department of Veterans Affairs (VA), more than 50,000 cases of PTSD have been diagnosed during the Operation Iraqi Freedom and Operation Enduring Freedom conflicts (Ephron, 2007). Treatment options include counseling to help servicemembers develop coping skills, support groups, and antidepressant medication.

NEW DIRECTIONS FOR STUDENT SERVICES • DOI: 10.1002/ss

The service-related disabilities described in this section, or combinations thereof, are illustrative of the types of issues that students who are disabled veterans may bring to the campus and the classroom. Higher education professionals should be familiar with the challenges that this new generation of war-wounded veterans may face. How best to support these veterans is still being debated, but this chapter details one project that has demonstrated promise in establishing students on a trajectory for success. Hopefully, the initiative described here will serve as an example for the campus community, including central administration leaders, academic affairs personnel, and student services professionals.

An Initiative for Serving Injured Veterans

Severely Injured Military Veterans: Fulfilling Their Dream is an initiative of the American Council on Education (ACE) and is funded by private contributors (American Council on Education, 2008a). The project, begun in April 2007, is designed to ensure that severely wounded veterans and their families receive support as they make the transition from wartime service to postsecondary education. Program staff and volunteers have assisted more than 400 servicemembers and veterans with their postwar goals; this assistance has often involved finding postsecondary programs that will help them meet their goals. Seventy-eight veterans are currently enrolled or accepted at a variety of higher education institutions. As of the summer of 2008, thirteen have completed postsecondary programs. This early success is due, in part, to the hard work and dedication of the staff and volunteers who support the program.

Since 1918, ACE has provided leadership and a unified voice on key higher education issues (American Council on Education, 2008b). Through advocacy, research, and innovative programs, ACE represents the interests of more than 1,800 campus executives, as well as the leaders of higher education associations and organizations. Together, ACE member institutions serve 80 percent of today's college students. ACE speaks as higher education's voice in matters of public policy in Washington, D.C., and throughout the nation and provides vital programs, information, and a forum for dialogue on key issues. The National Association of Student Personnel Administrators (NASPA) has partnered with ACE to help severely injured veterans find a mentor at the college or university they plan to attend. With more than 11,000 members representing 1,400 institutions, NASPA can provide a point of contact at a majority of the schools of interest to veterans from the program.

Support from the ACE program starts while the injured servicemember is recovering at a military hospital such as Walter Reed Army Medical Center, Bethesda Naval Hospital, Brooke Army Hospital, or the Naval Medical Center San Diego. There is an ACE academic advisor at each hospital. The advisor assists each client in developing an individual educational plan. This unique group of student veterans aspires to a full spectrum of educational goals, from high school equivalency to graduate and postgraduate degrees.

A majority are seeking certificate programs, two-year degrees, or baccalaureate degrees. Participants may be first-generation students, first-time students, or returning students.

ACE staff found that veterans were disinclined to request assistance and, therefore, needed help finding information about a particular college's academic offerings, orientation program, and campus culture. Moreover, when a veteran is medically discharged or officially retired, he or she may not qualify to receive continued support from and access to Department of Defense or VA education services. Therefore, through ACE program staff and with the assistance of NASPA members, veterans are connected with volunteer mentors known as *champions*. According to the description provided on the ACE Web site (American Council on Education, 2008a), a champion

- Invests time and energy to help the veteran make informed decisions
- Provides guidance for dealing with the chaos of college and assists in bridging the gap from the military's mission-oriented structure to an academic environment
- Serves as a resource to assist with matters such as study skills, tutoring support services, veterans affairs issues, and enrollment challenges
- Seeks to build a community-based team of support for the veteran or family member (or both)
- Needs to be flexible and persevere because the veteran or family member will undoubtedly face setbacks and obstacles on his or her journey, particularly when getting started

Champions, or mentors, can be fellow students, faculty members, or administrators and are often veterans themselves. Campus advocacy by the mentor can be essential in initiating access to resources needed to provide assistance to a severely injured veteran. In addition to the champion, family members and other volunteers may also play an important role in helping a recovering veteran with the transition to college.

Student and Mentor Profiles

The following profiles, intended to be representative of students and mentors from the ACE program, are offered to the reader for illustrative purposes, with the intent to familiarize student services professionals with realistic examples. The profiles are based on actual events and genuine participants in the program, but names and identifying information have been changed to protect privacy.

Online Learning. Amanda joined the Army in 2004 and was deployed to Iraq in 2005. In 2006, she was severely injured when a truck loaded with propane exploded near her convoy. Amanda and other soldiers suffered extensive burns. She received treatment at Brooke Army Hospital, including many surgeries over an eighteen-month period and numerous hours of physical therapy. During her recovery, she enrolled in an online associate degree program in criminal justice. Amanda credited the ACE academic advisor at Brooke with helping her find a course of study that interested her, as well as assisting her in selecting and applying to an acceptable school. She plans to take a civilian job in law enforcement and continue her studies. Readers should note that online learning was the only practicable way for Amanda to begin and continue postsecondary study at the time, primarily due to frequent doctor's visits and rehabilitation appointments associated with her injuries.

Educational Goals That Aid Recovery. Michael served in the Army for more than four years and earned the rank of sergeant. Deployed to Iraq in 2005, he operated armored vehicles in a unit charged with protecting convoys. Just a few months into his deployment, as Michael was sitting in the passenger seat of a Humvee while returning from a successful convoy mission, a roadside bomb detonated next to the truck, causing significant damage and injury. Tragically, he lost his left leg in the explosion. Michael took treatment for nearly a year at Walter Reed Army Medical Center, where he received a prosthetic leg and participated in physical rehabilitation. A bright young man who showed academic promise, Michael worked with his ACE advisor at the hospital in order to begin online courses during his recovery, with the goal of transferring to a state university and studying for a career in a health-related profession. He has since made the transition to civilian life and is attending university classes. Coordinating with Michael's ACE advisor, a NASPA volunteer contacted the chief student affairs officer at Michael's university prior to his arrival. The chief student affairs officer, in turn, notified appropriate campus personnel, including staff members in veterans affairs and disability services, to assist Michael with his academic journey. While he never actually received an individual mentor, the group effort and support from a cadre of campus personnel has proven successful. Michael plans to finish a baccalaureate degree at the university and pursue graduate school thereafter. His story illustrates how pursuing higher education can provide a positive focus during a veteran's recovery and transition.

A Desire to Give Back. Adam served in the Marine Corps in Iraq, beginning in early 2006. In 2007, while he was returning to base from a mission in Fallujah, an IED exploded under the vehicle carrying him, resulting in severe leg injuries. Sadly, his left leg required amputation and his right foot required extensive reconstructive surgery. He eventually spent one year at Brooke Army Hospital to receive treatment for his injuries and heal. Adam had completed two years of college prior to joining the military. With the assistance of the ACE academic advisor at the hospital, he is now pursuing a baccalaureate degree at a university in his home state. Adam's goal is to finish school and work in the medical equipment industry, particularly in prosthetics, where he can use his personal experience and expertise to help others. Adam wants to use his educational benefits to earn a degree and work in a field where he can give back to others who have been injured.

A Mentor Who Served in Iraq. Carl is an administrator in student affairs at a large East Coast university. He is also a retired colonel in the Army Reserves and did a tour in Iraq in 2005 and 2006. Through a referral from the vice president for student affairs at his university, Carl got a call from the NASPA liaison, who was seeking a mentor for a severely injured veteran, Chris, from the ACE program. Chris was newly admitted and could use the help. Carl readily agreed to meet with him and see how things progressed from there. Due in part to their common military experiences, the two veterans got along well and met regularly for a while to ensure that Carl's protégé got a solid start in school. Since then, two semesters have passed and they see each other less frequently now. However, the initial support and advocacy provided by Carl was important.

A Bridge to Peer Support. Daniel, an academic dean at a Midwestern university and a former Marine, was an ideal candidate for mentoring a severely injured veteran from the ACE program. When the volunteer liaison from NASPA called about the opportunity to be a champion for Tony in the program, he agreed without hesitation. Daniel's military background helped him build rapport with Tony, but his position in both academics and administration proved invaluable in helping his protégé deal with bureaucratic hurdles, seek out educational advice, and obtain referrals to people who could provide support in regard to the emotional aspects of a transition to civilian life. Perhaps most important, Daniel introduced Tony to the student veterans organization on campus (see Chapter Eight). In this case, peer support appears to be the critical factor in student success. While his role as a mentor diminished over time, Daniel's initial support for the student from the ACE program was vital.

Feedback from Students and Mentors

Several veterans participating in the ACE program mentioned the presence of uncontrollable variables that acted as barriers to pursuing an academic lifestyle and regular class attendance. These obstacles included rehabilitation appointments, ongoing disputes with the military medical review board, and physical setbacks that required follow-up surgeries. Perhaps these factors explain the popularity of online distance learning courses among this student population (Field, 2008). Program participants also reported difficulty in making the transition to civilian life and school, often simply because of timing factors and changing plans. However, the ACE academic advisor at the hospital not only assists with matters of timing but, perhaps most important, also helps the severely injured servicemember identify his or her own academic and professional interests, as well as determine which type of institution best fits his or her needs (for example, a community college, a university, or an online program).

NEW DIRECTIONS FOR STUDENT SERVICES • DOI: 10.1002/ss

Difficulties associated with memory loss and confusion related to information overload were also noted as impediments to college attendance, according to several of the veterans in the program. These hindrances to student success can be exacerbated by a reluctance to seek assistance. One student demonstrated an inability to complete necessary paperwork and could not explain why, which is a type of experience that is sometimes associated with PTSD. When problems of this sort occur, the mentorship arranged through the ACE program can be a valuable source of support and guidance. For example, a mentor from the program requested information about how a military security clearance would be affected if a disabled veteran sought psychological counseling for PTSD. Interestingly, several student veterans from the program are interested in pursuing careers in military intelligence and have concerns about their health record. These privacy issues also give rise to concerns about registering for a documented learning disability, including college course accommodations for memory difficulties associated with TBI.

A number of the mentors cited their primary role as a resource to help veterans find answers and get the help they needed. One noted that just offering the extra support bolstered the confidence of the disabled student in his charge. When a student voiced concern about acceptance in college, mostly due to being an older student and attending an institution that was known for a predominance of liberal views, his mentor offered to assist him in getting involved with the student veterans organization on campus. The notion that peer support is key for student success is well documented in research findings, starting with Astin (1977) more than thirty years ago, and is still true today for the severely injured veterans in the ACE program.

Concluding Thoughts

While Severely Injured Military Veterans: Fulfilling Their Dream, the American Council on Education's initiative, is relatively new and still developing, the successes achieved by participating veterans are inspiring. Not surprisingly, for a severely injured veteran, pursuit of postsecondary education can provide a focal point for rebuilding a shattered life. In a sense, this is a type of rehabilitation that occurs beyond the hospital setting; furthermore, a positive transition to civilian life is an intrinsic part of this type of rehabilitation. However, if a student's dream of college attendance is threatened by bureaucratic red tape, feelings of rejection by classmates and faculty members, or physical and psychological limitations, the prospect of failure can be devastating. These pitfalls are why assistance from an academic advisor from ACE, coordination with a NASPA volunteer liaison, and support from a champion at the veteran's new institution are vital. Because no single model for support is sufficient to meet each unique student's needs, a team approach like the ACE program is required to ensure success.

References

American Council on Education. "Severely Injured Military Veterans: Fulfilling Their Dream." [http://www.acenet.edu/Content/NavigationMenu/ProgramsServices/Military Programs/veterans/index.htm]. 2008a. Retrieved Nov. 12, 2008.

American Council on Education. "Who We Are." [http://www.acenet.edu/Content/ NavigationMenu/About/WhoWeAre/who_we_are.htm]. 2008b. Retrieved Nov. 12, 2008.

Astin, A. W. Four Critical Years: Effects of College on Beliefs, Attitudes, and Knowledge. San Francisco: Jossey-Bass, 1977.

Cohen, D. Undefeated: The Life of Hubert H. Humphrey. Minneapolis, Minn.: Lerner, 1978.

Emmons, M. "Traumatic Brain Injury: The 'Signature Wound' of Wars in Iraq and Afghanistan." Oakland Tribune. [http://nl.newsbank.com/nl-search/we/Archives= 113840p]. Dec. 26, 2006. Retrieved Nov. 12, 2008.

Ephron, D. "Forgotten Heroes." Newsweek, Mar. 5, 2007, pp. 29–37.

Field, K. "Cost, Convenience Drive Veterans' College Choices." Chronicle of Higher Education, July 25, 2008, 54(46), A1.

iCasualties.org. "U.S. Wounded in Iraq" [http://icasualties.org/oif/]. 2008. Retrieved Nov. 15, 2008.

Kinchin, D. Post Traumatic Stress Disorder: The Invisible Injury. Oxfordshire, U.K.: Success Unlimited, 2005.

Stiglitz, J., and Bilmes, L. The Three Trillion Dollar War: The True Cost of the Iraq Conflict. New York: Norton, 2008.

Zoroya, G. "Military Prodded on Brain Injuries." USA Today, [http://www.usatoday.com/ news/washington/2007–03–07-brain-injuries_N.htm]. Mar. 3, 2007. Retrieved Nov. 12, 2008.

DAVID DIRAMIO is assistant professor of higher education administration at Auburn University.

MICHELE SPIRES is assistant director for military programs at the American Council on Education.

NEW DIRECTIONS FOR STUDENT SERVICES • DOI: 10.1002/ss

10

This chapter describes the federal laws and policies that affect enrollment and retention of servicemembers, veterans, and their dependents in higher education institutions, providing campus administrators with an essential reference.

Stewards of the Public Trust: Federal Laws That Serve Servicemembers and Student Veterans

Michael McGrevey, Darryl Kehrer

Student services professionals are committed to helping students, including the new generation of military servicemembers. However, navigating the maze of federal programs and policies designed to help these deserving individuals requires special knowledge. This chapter assists campus administrators by providing information, first, on the rich history of federal programs and policies that servicemembers and veterans use in pursuing higher education and, second, on how to access these services and entitlement benefits through the federal agencies that administer them.

Why the United States Assists Its Military Veterans

Federal veterans benefits are as old as the republic. The British colonies in North America furnished pensions to disabled veterans. Enacted in 1636 by Plymouth Colony, the same year as the founding of Harvard College, pensions provided money to the militiamen disabled in the colony's defense against Native Americans; other colonies followed Plymouth Colony's lead (U.S. Department of Veterans Affairs, 1997). Such policies endured: "In 1776 the Continental Congress sought to encourage enlistments and curtail desertions with the nation's first pension law. Later, grants of public land were made to those who served to the end of the war" (U.S. Department of Veterans Affairs, 1997, p. 2). Later, the Homestead Act gave veterans of the Union Army priority in purchasing Western lands (U.S. Department of Veterans Affairs, 1997).

NEW DIRECTIONS FOR STUDENT SERVICES, no. 126, Summer 2009 © Wiley Periodicals, Inc.
Published online in Wiley InterScience (www.interscience.wiley.com) • DOI: 10.1002/ss.320

With respect to more contemporary benefits that are specific to education and training, since World War II, some 21 million veterans have used the various educational assistance programs popularly known as the GI Bill that have produced inestimable numbers of teachers, engineers, physicians, lawyers, bankers, entrepreneurs, and others. Over the generations, these adult learners have brought maturity, academic achievement, and leadership to campus (Mettler, 2005). Following is an outline of education-related federal programs designed to compensate those who serve in the military. An understanding of these programs is essential for campus administrators who are responsible for assisting veterans.

Federal Benefits for Active-Duty Military and Members of the National Guard and Reserves

The Tuition Assistance (TA) program, codified at 10 U.S.C. § 2007, is a long-standing program administered by the Department of Defense. TA furnishes servicemembers with up to $4,500 annually to voluntarily pursue a college degree during off-duty time. Funded by Congress at $465 million in fiscal year 2007, some 800,000 servicemembers pursued degrees through TA, earning 25,800 associate's degrees, 10,484 bachelor's degrees, 2,666 master's degrees, 110 high school or general equivalency degrees, and 10 doctoral degrees (Baker, 2008).

Higher Education Relief Opportunities for Students (HEROES) Act of 2003 (Public Law 108-76, approved on August 18, 2003). HEROES and subsequent amendments furnish financial protections to active-duty servicemembers, National Guard members, and reservists who receive federal student financial aid and serve in the U.S. military during a war, military operation, or national emergency. Congress essentially made HEROES permanent in Public Law 110-93 (approved on September 30, 2007), furnishing the Secretary of Education with broad authority to issue waivers and modify various statutory and regulatory provisions related to financial aid to affected servicemembers. These provisions were designed to not place servicemembers in a worse position financially due to their military service. HEROES provides specific relief to activated servicemembers who are repaying student loans. According to a regulation of December 19, 2007, the secretary's waivers of statute and regulation will remain in effect until September 30, 2012 (U.S. Department of Education, 2007).

The Servicemembers Civil Relief Act (SCRA) (Public Law 108-189, approved on December 9, 2003). Formerly known as the Soldiers' and Sailors' Civil Relief Act of 1940, SCRA modernizes earlier legislation by providing various financial, civil, and legal protections to servicemembers, including National Guard members, as they are called to active duty (American Bar Association, 2006). In late 2004, Congress fine-tuned SCRA in Public Law 108-454, approved on December 10, 2004 (American Bar Association, 2006). College staff who counsel deploying students will want to note that

SCRA furnishes protections in financial matters such as "rental agreements, security deposits, prepaid rent, eviction, credit card interest rates, mortgage foreclosure, insurance and tax payments" (U.S. Department of Justice, 2008, p. 1). On-campus application of SCRA typically applies to active-duty service-members who are pursuing off-duty degrees, members of the reserve forces and National Guard who are pursuing full-time or part-time degrees, and the institution's own faculty and staff who are members of the National Guard or reserves.

Uniformed Services Employment and Reemployment Rights Act (USERRA) of 1994 (Public Law 103-353, approved on October 13, 1994). Initially enacted as part of the Selective Training and Service Act of 1940 (U.S. Department of Veterans Affairs, 1995), USERRA protects both the civilian job rights and employee benefits of veterans and members of the National Guard or reserves. With respect to the college population, USERRA furnishes employment protections to students, faculty, and staff who are called to active duty:

> USERRA provides that returning service-members [sic] are reemployed in the job that they *would* [emphasis added] have attained had they not been absent for military service (the longstanding "escalator" principle), with the same seniority, status and pay, as well as other rights and benefits determined by seniority. USERRA also requires that reasonable efforts (such as training or retraining) be made to enable returning servicemembers [sic] to refresh or upgrade their skills to help qualify them for reemployment. The law clearly provides for alternative reemployment positions if the servicemember [sic] cannot qualify for the "escalator" position. (U.S. Department of Labor, 2008, p. 1)

For servicemembers in general, Congress established the Transition Assistance Program (TAP) as a pilot program in 1990. Congress codified TAP in the National Defense Authorization Act for Fiscal Year 1991 (U.S. Department of Veterans Affairs, 2007). The in-person assistance generally known as a TAP typically requires attendance at a three-day workshop. The Department of Defense furnishes pre-separation counseling; the Department of Labor furnishes USERRA briefings and job placement help; and the Department of Veterans Affairs furnishes briefings on veterans benefits as well as specific help for disabled veterans (U.S. Department of Defense, 2007). Campus administrators may find the front-loaded nature of TAP services useful for the college admissions process in that, by law, active-duty servicemembers are encouraged to access TAP services twelve months prior to separation or twenty-four months prior to retirement (U.S. Department of Defense, 2007).

Montgomery and Post-9/11 GI Bill Programs

Some 2.3 million veterans have pursued postsecondary education and training through the Montgomery GI Bill (MGIB) (Public Law 100-48, approved

June 1, 1987). Veterans who pursue full-time, college-level training under the MGIB—Active Duty program receive $1,321 per month as of August 1, 2008, for up to thirty-six months or four academic years; have ten years to use benefits; and agree to a pay reduction of $100 per month over the first twelve months of military service to become eligible. Approximately 71 percent of active-duty personnel take advantage of MGIB. Members of the National Guard and reserves pursuing college-level training under the MGIB—Selected Reserve program generally receive $329 per month and must remain in the reserves to use the program but have no $1,200 pay reduction. Members of the National Guard and the reserves in many states may also use Tuition Assistance benefits.

Congress established a new Post-9/11 GI Bill on June 30, 2008, as part of the 2008 Supplemental Appropriation Act (Public Law 110-252). The Post-9/11 GI Bill takes effect on August 1, 2009. Veterans who pursue college-level training at the associate degree level or higher will receive tuition and fees, paid directly to the institution, not to exceed the cost of the most expensive in-state public institution of higher education. A monthly living/housing allowance is included, equal to the local rate of the basic allowance for housing for a married, military E-5 (junior noncommissioned officer). Other provisions include a yearly $1,000 stipend for books and supplies and a one-time payment of $500 if the veteran relocates from a highly rural area. The veteran will have fifteen years to use thirty-six months (four academic years) of entitlement. No reduction in basic pay is required for participation in the Post-9/11 program. Servicemembers serving on or after August 1, 2009, and who agree to serve for specified additional periods, may be able to transfer benefits to a spouse or dependent child (U.S. Department of Veterans Affairs, 2008).

Other Veterans' Benefits

The Veterans Administration (VA) administers a vocational rehabilitation and employment program for certain service-disabled veterans, as well as a survivors' and dependents' education program for families of servicemembers who die in service or veterans who have a permanent and total service-connected disability rating from the VA. All users of VA educational assistance programs are eligible for vocational/educational counseling and testing services from the VA. Plus, the VA maintains 232 community-based veterans centers nationwide that furnish specialized assistance to combat veterans.

For state-administered veterans benefits, the privately published *For Service to Your Country: The Insider's Guide to Veterans' Benefits* (Gaytan and Border, 2008) is an excellent source of information on state and federal benefits alike. This publication furnishes the contact information for state agencies that administer veterans benefits. In addition, campus administrators can follow federal legislative developments on the Web site of the U.S. House of Representatives' Committee on Veterans' Affairs (see Appendix).

Concluding Thoughts

Military servicemembers and veterans make a valuable addition to any student population because they bring unique experiences and skills to campus. During a House Committee on Veterans' Affairs press conference, Representative Henry Brown of South Carolina asked rhetorically, "In what other aspects of our society do technology-savvy 20-year-olds maintain multi-million-dollar tactical aircraft, navigate and troubleshoot multi-billion-dollar nuclear-powered ships, and operate and maintain space-based technologies to keep us safe in an increasingly unsafe world?" (Brown, 2004, p. 1). Deployed to some 120 countries around the world, U.S. servicemembers often see firsthand the effects of political injustice and tyranny. A 2005 national study of confidence in leadership found that Americans have more confidence in the leaders in their professional, all-volunteer military than in any other profession in American society (Yankelovich, Inc., 2005). U.S. servicemembers' resolute service on the world stage, combined with the 523,000 beneficiaries currently enrolled under the Montgomery GI Bill, vocational rehabilitation, and surviving spouses' and dependents' education programs, makes veterans and their families a population that adds value, bringing leadership, experience, and know-how to campus.

Appendix: Web Sites

- GI Bill Programs. http://www.gibill.va.gov
- HEROES. http://www.finaid.org/military/heroes.phtml and http://www.ed.gov/legislation/fedRegister/proprule/2007-4/122607a
- House Committee on Veterans' Affairs. http://www.veterans.house.gov
- SCRA. http://www.military.com/benefits/legal-matters/scra/overview and http://abanet.org/legalservices/lamp/downloads/SCRAguide.pdf
- Transition Assistance Program. http://www.turbotap.org
- Tuition Assistance Program. http://armyu.com/public/tuitionassistance_policies.aspx and http://www.voled.doded.mil
- USERRA. http://www.dol.gov/vets/programs/userra/userra_fs.htm
- Vet Centers. http://www.vetcenter.va.gov
- Vocational-Educational Counseling. http://www.vba.gov/bln/bre/vec.htm
- Vocational Rehabilitation and Dependents' Education Programs. http://www.vba.va.gov/VBA

References

American Bar Association. "The Servicemembers Civil Relief Act Guide, 2006." American Bar Association. [http://abanet.org/legalservices/lamp/downloads/SCRAguide.pdf]. 2006. Retrieved July 8, 2008.

Baker, C. "DoD Voluntary Education: A Broad Overview, Fiscal Year 2007 Update." Department of Defense. [http://www.voled.dod.mil]. 2008. Retrieved July 2, 2008.

Brown, H. "Wall Street and Main Street Agree: Veterans Give Businesses the Winning Edge." Press conference for the House Committee on Veterans' Affairs, Washington, D.C. [http://veterans.house.gov/hearings/schedule108/mar04/3-24-04/witness.html]. Mar. 24, 2004. Retrieved Dec. 9, 2008.

Gaytan, P. S., and Border, M. E. *For Service to Your Country: The Insider's Guide to Veterans' Benefits.* Charleston, S.C.: Citadel Press, 2008.

Mettler, S. B. *Soldiers to Citizens: The G.I. Bill and the Making of the Greatest Generation.* Oxford, U.K.: Oxford University Press, 2005.

Public Law 100-48. "Montgomery GI Bill." [http://www.uscg.mil/directives/ci/1000-1999/CI_1001_30E.pdf]. 1987. Retrieved Dec. 19, 2008.

Public Law 103-353. "Uniformed Services Employment and Reemployment Rights Act." [http://www.opm.gov/retire/pubs/bals/1995/95-101.pdf]. 1994. Retrieved Dec. 19, 2008.

Public Law 108-76. "Higher Education Relief Opportunities for Students." [http://bulk.resource.org/gpo.gov/laws/108/publ076.108.txt]. 2003. Retrieved Dec. 19, 2008.

Public Law 108-189. "The Servicemembers Civil Relief Act." [http://bulk.resource.org/gpo.gov/laws/108/publ189.108.txt]. 2003. Retrieved Dec. 19, 2008.

Public Law 108-454. "Veterans Benefits Improvement Act of 2004." [http://bulk.resource.org/gpo.gov/laws/108/publ454.108.txt]. 2004. Retrieved Dec. 19, 2008.

Public Law 110-93. "110th Congress: An Act." [http://www.nchelp.org/elibrary/BudgetReconciliation&HEAReauthorization/2007HEALegislation/StatutoryMaterials/PL110-093.pdf]. 2007. Retrieved Dec. 19, 2008.

Public Law 110-252. "2008 Supplemental Appropriation Act: Post-9/11 GI Bill." [http://frwebgate.access.gpo.gov/cgi-bin/getdoc.cgi?dbname=110_cong_bills&docid=f:h2642enr.txt.pdf]. 2008. Retrieved Dec. 19, 2008.

U.S. Department of Defense. "Transition Assistance Program Preseparation Guide: Active Duty, 2007." [http://www.TurboTAP.org]. 2007. Retrieved July 2, 2008.

U.S. Department of Education. "Federal Student Aid Programs." *Federal Register,* 72(246), 72947–72948. [http://www.ed.gov/legislation/FedRegister/proprule/2007-4/122607a.html]. 2007. Retrieved Oct. 13, 2008.

U.S. Department of Justice. "Servicemembers Civil Relief Act: Safeguarding the Rights of Servicemembers and Veterans." [http://www.justice.gov/crt/military/scratext.html]. 2008. Retrieved July 7, 2008.

U.S. Department of Labor. "VETS USERRA Fact Sheet 3: Job Rights for Veterans and Reserve Component Members." Veterans Employment and Training Service. [http://www.dol.gov/vets/programs/userra/userra_fs.htm]. 2008. Retrieved June 18, 2008.

U.S. Department of Veterans Affairs. *The Veterans Benefits Administration: An Organizational History: 1776–1994.* Washington, D.C.: Veterans Benefits Administration, 1995.

U.S. Department of Veterans Affairs. *VA History in Brief.* Washington, D.C.: U.S. Government Printing Office, 1997.

U.S. Department of Veterans Affairs. "Seamless Transition: Transition Assistance Information for Enduring Freedom and Iraqi Freedom Veterans." [http://www.seamlesstransition.va.gov/transition.asp]. 2007. Retrieved June 18, 2008.

U.S. Department of Veterans Affairs. "The Post-9/11 Veterans Education Assistance Act of 2008." [http://www.gibill.va.gov]. 2008. Retrieved July 5, 2008.

Yankelovich, Inc. "National Leadership Index 2005: A National Study of Confidence in Leadership." *U.S. News & World Report.* [http://www.usnews.com/usnews/news/features/051022/22/leaders.pdf]. October 18, 2005. Retrieved Oct. 12, 2008.

MICHAEL MCGREVEY, *an Air Force veteran, is vice president for finance and administration at Mississippi State University.*

DARRYL KEHRER, *an Air Force veteran, is policy officer for the G. V. Montgomery Center for America's Veterans at Mississippi State University.*

INDEX

Abes, E. S., 39, 41
Abrams, R. M., 26
ACE. *See* American Council on Education (ACE)
Ackerman, R., 5, 30
Advisory Council on Military Education, 67
Afghanistan, conflict in, 12, 13, 35–38, 72
African American students, 30
Alcohol abuse issues, 13
Allen, E., 64
Allen, W., 72
American Association of Community Colleges, 63
American Association of State Colleges and Universities, 63
American Bar Association, 90
American Council on Education (ACE), 48, 83–87
American Legion, 51, 52
American military system, 26
American Veterans Committee, 71
Americans with Disabilities Act, 13
Anger, problems with, 13, 38, 66
Anti-military activism, 26
Anti-war activism, 26
Anxiety, 38, 46
Anxiety disorder, 82
Appalachian State University, 55–60; Web site, 58
Appalachian, The, 58
Army/American Council on Education Registry Transcript Service, 9
Asch, B. J., 26–28
Astin, A. W., 87
Auchterlonie, J. L., 13, 17

Baechtold, M., 35
Baker, C., 62, 90
Baker, H., 35, 36
Bauman, M., 15
Baxter Magolda, M. B., 38
BCT. *See* U.S. Army:1/34 Brigade Combat Team
Bertenthal, D., 13
Bethesda Naval Hospital, 83
Beyond the Yellow Ribbon program, 46, 47

Bilmes, L., 81
Blankenship, J., 37
Border, M. E., 93
Bosnia, peace keeping mission in, 47, 55
Bradley, K., 37
British colonies, 89
Brooke Army Hospital, 83–85
Brown, H., 93
Bush, K., 37

Camp Lejeune, 55
Camp Shelby, Mississippi, 18
Campus support services, 9
Campus veterans services offices, 9
Carroll, A., 72
Castro, C. A., 46
Champions, 84
Chickering, A. W., 40
China, war in, 31
Clayton-Pederson, A., 72
Cognitive problems, 82
Cohen, D., 81
Cohen, S., 13
Cold War, post-Vietnam, 72
Collison, M., 28
Combat fatigue, 82
Combat veterans, as college students: and deployment, 6–7; discussion and conclusions concerning, 12–13; emergent themes regarding, 3; and joining military, 6; and re-entering civilian life and becoming student, 10–12; and serving in war zone, 7–8; and transition from combat to classroom, 8–12
Congress, 90
Corbett, S., 13
Cotting, D. I., 46
Council of College and Military Educators, 63, 67
Cozza, S. J., 46
Creswell, J. W., 5

Davis, M., 30
Davis, T., 37
De Sawal, D. M., 35
DeBenedetti, C., 71
Defense Activity for Non-Traditional Educational Support, 63, 67
Defense Manpower Data Center, 12, 46

Deitrick, A. L., 37
DeLoughry, T. J., 28
"Department of Defense FY07 Report on Sexual Assault in the Military" (U.S. Department of Defense), 38
Department of Defense Worldwide, 63
Deployed students: continued connection of, 58–59; and enhancing and improving support for student veterans, 59–60; ensuring success of, 55–60; and making transition from student to active-duty soldier, 55–58; and transition from military duty to student life, 59
Depression, 13, 38, 46
Desert Shield Support Group, 58
Dias-Bowie, Y., 30
DiRamio, D., 5, 30, 81
Disabled Veterans of America, 51
Dobie, D., 37
Dodge, S., 28
Doubler, M. D., 27

Eglin Air Force Base, 61
Emmons, M., 82
Engel, C. C., 46
Ephron, D., 82

FAFSA. See Free Application for Federal Student Aid (FAFSA)
Fair, C. C., 26
Fallujah, Iraq, 85
Federal laws, 89–93; and federal benefits for active-duty military and members on National Guard and reserves, 90–91; and Montgomery and Post-9/11 GI Bill programs, 91–92; and reason United States assists its military veterans, 89–90
Federal Student Handbook, 56
Ferguson, Brigadier General Michael L., 63–64
Field, K., 86
Florida Advisory Council on Military Education, 63
Ford, D., 61
Fort Bragg, 55
Foster, A., 31
Frayne, S., 38
Free Application for Federal Student Aid (FAFSA), 50–51

Gaytan, P. S., 92
Gender identity, 36
GI Bill (Servicemen's Readjustment Act), 20, 26, 32, 50, 56, 57, 71, 77, 78, 90

Glass, J. C., 16
Goodman, J., 12
Green, S.-M., 71
Greenberg, K., 30
Grieger, T. A., 46
Griffith, J., 15
Gruber, C. S., 26
"Guard-On-Line" (Minnesota State Colleges and Universities System), 47
Gulf War, 35, 59, 72

Hamrick, F. A., 25, 29, 30
Hankin, C. S., 38
Harshberger, R. F., 16
Harvard College, 89
Herbert, M. S., 39, 40
HEROES. See Higher Education Relief Opportunities for Students Act (HEROES; Public Law 108–76)
Higher Education Reintegration Training Team, 47
Higher Education Relief Opportunities for Students Act (HEROES; Public Law 108–76), 90
Higher Education Veterans Assistance Program (Minnesota Statute 197.585), 47
Hoge, C. W., 13, 17, 46
Homestead Act, 89
Hometown Heroes Teach (University of West Florida), 64–65
Horan, M., 26
Hoyt, J. E., 16
Humphrey, Hubert H., 81
Hunt, A. E., 72
Hunter, A., 64
Hurlburt Field, 61
Hurricane Katrina, 6, 27
Hurtado, S., 72

iCasualties.org, 82
Indiana University, 77; Vet Club, 74
Iraq, conflict in, 12, 13, 17, 31, 35–38, 46, 72, 81, 84–86

Jarhead (Swofford), 31
Jin, H., 31
Johnson, T., 55
Jones, S. R., 39, 41
Josselson, R., 40

Kansas Collegiate Veterans Association, 77
Kasworm, C. E., 16
Keeling, R., 68

Kehrer, D., 89
Kilburn, M. R., 26, 27
Kinchin, D., 82
Kinzie, J., 13
Kivlahan, D., 37
Klerman, J. A., 27
Klukken, G., 30
Koffman, R. I., 46
Konkle-Parker, D. J., 15
Korean War, 71, 81
Korean War era, 26, 27
Kressin, N., 38
Kuh, G. D., 13

Lanigan, K., 67
Learning Reconsidered (Keeling), 68
Listman, J. W., 33
Litz, B. T., 35–36
Lokken, J. M., 45
Lorge, E. M., 46
Loughran, D., 27, 28

Marcia, J. E., 40
Marmar, C., 13
Martinez, P. E., 46
Maynard, C., 37
McAuley, J., 45
McEwen, M. K., 38, 39, 41
McGrevey, M., 89
McGurk, D., 46
MDVA. *See* Minnesota Department of Veterans Affairs (MDVA)
Mental health problems, 13, 21, 36–38
Messer, S. C., 46
Mettler, S. B., 90
MGIB. *See* Montgomery GI Bill (MGIB)
Middle East, 63
Mikelson, J., 28–29
Milem, J., 72
Military Connections Committee (University of West Florida), 65, 66
Military sexual trauma, 37
Military.com, 27
Miller, D. R., 38
Milliken, C. S., 13, 17
Mills, D., 46
Miner, C. R., 13
Minnesota Department of Employment and Economic Development, 51
Minnesota Department of Veterans Affairs (MDVA), 47; Higher Education Veterans Programs, 45, 47, 48, 50–53
Minnesota GI Bill, 51
Minnesota National Guard (MNANG), 46, 47

Minnesota Office of Higher Education, 45, 47, 48
Minnesota Online, 49
Minnesota Private College Council, 47
Minnesota State Colleges and Universities System (MnSCU), 45, 47–49; Board of Trustees Policy 5.12, 50
Minnesota, state of, 46, 47–48, 53
Minnesota Statute 197.585 (Higher Education Veterans Assistance Program), 47
Minnesota Statute 197.775 (Higher Education Fairness), 47
Mississippi State University, 76–77
Mitchell, R., 5, 30
MnSCU. *See* Minnesota State Colleges and Universities System (MnSCU)
Montgomery GI Bill (MGIB; Public Law 100–48), 26, 91–93
Morrill Act (1862), 26
Morris, John, 46

NASPA. *See* National Association of Student Personnel Administrators (NASPA)
National Association of Student Personnel Administrators (NASPA), 65, 83–87
National Association of Veterans' Program Administrators, 60
National Center for Posttraumatic Stress Disorder, 37–38
National Defense Act (NDA), 26
National Defense Authorization Act for Fiscal Year 1991, 91
National Guard, 7, 9, 12, 18, 25–28, 32, 46, 47, 50, 56, 62, 90–92
National Institute of Standards and Technology, 28
Native Americans, war against, 89
Naval Medical Center San Diego, 83
NDA. *See* National Defense Act (NDA)
Neiberg, M. S., 25
New Orleans, Louisiana, 6
Noddings, N., 31
North Carolina Association of Coordinators of Veterans Affairs, 60
Northrup, P., 61

O'Brien, T., 31
O'Bryant, J., 15
Ocean of Words (Jin), 31
O'Herrin, Elizabeth, 67
Okaloosa County, Florida, 63–64
Olson, K. W., 26

Online learning, 84–85
Operation Desert Shield, 55–58; Support Group, 58
Operation Desert Storm, 28, 55–58
Operation Enduring Freedom, 28, 55, 82
Operation Iraqi Freedom, 28, 55, 82
Operation Noble Eagle, 28

Parker, D., 71
Parker, J. D., 15
Partnering: to assist disabled veterans in transition, 81–87; and desire to give back, 85–86; and education goals that aid recovery, 85
Pell Grant, 28
Pensacola, Florida, 61
Pensacola Naval Air Station, 61
Pensacola Young Professionals Association, 62
Perconte, S. T., 37
Persian Gulf War, 28, 55, 59
Pfeffer, D. S., 45, 47
Plymouth Colony, 89
Pollio, H. R., 30
Pontius, E. B., 37
Pope Air Force Base, 55
Post 9/11 GI Bill, 27, 91–92
Post-traumatic stress disorder (PTSD), 10, 13, 17, 21, 36–37, 46, 65, 66, 81, 82, 87
Pre-mobilization phase, of mobilization process, 16
PTSD. See Post-traumatic stress disorder (PTSD)
Public Law 100–48 (Montgomery GI Bill), 91–92
Public Law 103–353 (Uniformed Services Employment and Reemployment Rights Act), 91
Public Law 108–76 (Higher Education Relief Opportunities for Students Act), 90
Public Law 108–189 (Servicemembers Civil Relief Act), 90
Public Law 108–454, 90
Public Law 110–93, 90
Public Law 110–252 (Supplemental Appropriation Act, 2008), 92

Redden, E., 41
Reeves, R. R., 15
Rehabilitation Act of 1973 (Section 504), 13
Reisser, L., 40

Reserve forces, 25–28, 32, 56
Reserve Officers' Training Corps (ROTC), 26, 28, 30–31, 64, 65, 72, 73
Return phase, of mobilization process, 16
Richie, Colonel, 46
ROTC. See Reserve Officers' Training Corps (ROTC)
Rumann, C. B., 25, 29, 30
Ryan, D., 38

Sachs, R., 65
Saxe, R. E., 71
Schlossberg, N. K., 12
Schuh, J. H., 13
SCRA. See Public Law 108–189); Servicemembers Civil Relief Act (SCRA)
SCSU. See St. Cloud State University (SCSU)
SDRC. See Student Disability Resource Center (SDRC; University of West Florida)
Seal, K. H., 13
Seaman, J., 64
Selective Service System (SSS), 27
Selective Training and Service Act of 1940 (U.S. Department of Veterans Affairs), 91
Sen, S., 13
Separation phase, of mobilization process, 16
September 11 terrorist attacks, 27, 46, 55, 72
Service to Your Country: The Insider's Guide to Veterans' Benefits (Gaytan and Border), 92
Servicemembers Civil Relief Act (SCRA; Public Law 108–189), 90–91
Servicemembers Opportunity Colleges, 29, 63, 67
Servicemen's Readjustment Act (GI Bill; 1944), 26. See also GI Bill (Servicemen's Readjustment Act)
Severely Injured Military Veterans: Fulfilling Their Dream initiative (American Council on Education): as bridge to peer support, 86; and desire to give back, 85–86; and educational goals that aid recovery, 85; feedback from students and mentors on, 86–87; as initiative for serving injured veterans, 83–84; and online learning, 84–85; and partnering to assist disabled veterans in transition, 81–87; student and mentor profile in, 84–86

Sexual assault, 13, 36
Seymour Johnson Air Force Base, 55
Shell shock, 82
Shellito, Major General L., 46
Shipton, J., 16
Simultaneous Membership Program, 28
Skinner, K. M., 38
Smith, A. M., 64
Smith, D. C., Jr., 25–26
Soldiers' and Sailors' Civil Relief Act of
    1940, 90
Sonny Montgomery Center for America's
    Veterans, Mississippi State University,
    76–77
Spires, M., 81
Spiro, K. J., 37
SSS. *See* Selective Service System (SSS)
St. Cloud State University (SCSU), 45,
    49–53; Student Veterans Organization
    (SVO), 45, 52; Veterans Task Force, 51
St. Cloud Veterans Affairs Medical Cen-
    ter, 51
Stafford, J., 13
State militias, 27
Steltenpohl, E., 16
Stiglitz, J., 81
Stone, A., 35, 36
Street, A., 13
Strong, C., 45
Student Disability Resource Center
    (SDRC; University of West Florida),
    66
Student veterans in transition, support-
    ing: and all-volunteer force and edu-
    cational incentives, 27; building
    awareness for, 31; and deployment
    patterns and implications for college
    enrollment, 28–29; and preparing sol-
    diers and educating veterans, 25–27;
    recommendations for, 31–32; relevant
    campus considerations for, 29–31
Student Veterans of America (SVA),
    28–29, 67, 78
Student veterans organizations, 71–79;
    and campus climate, 72–74; function
    of, 77–78; importance of, 74–75
Students' Army Training Corps, 26
Substance abuse, 38
Sullivan, L. M., 38
Summerlot, J., 71
Supplemental Appropriation Act, 2008
    (Public Law 110–252), 92
SVA. *See* Student Veterans of America
Swofford, A., 31

TA. *See* Tuition Assistance program
TAP. *See* Transition Assistance Program
    (TAP)
TBI. *See* Traumatic brain injury (TBI)
Things They Carried, The (O'Brien), 31
Thomas, S. P., 30
Thompson, C. L., 30
"Throttling down," 16
"Throttling up," 16
Toven, J. R., 26
Transition Assistance Program (TAP), 91
Traumatic brain injury (TBI), 81, 87
Tripp, T. J., 38
Tuition Assistance program (TA), 90

Undergraduate students serving in
    National Guards and reserves: dual
    roles of, 16–17; interviews with, 17–
    22; mobilization and return of, 15–22;
    and pre-mobilization phase, 17–18;
    and return phase, 20–22; and separa-
    tion phase, 18–20; suggestions for
    practice with, 22
Uniformed Services Employment and
    Reemployment Rights Act (USERRA;
    Public Law 103–353), 91
Union Army, 89
United States Army Reserve, 27
University of Indiana, 77
University of Iowa, 28–29
University of Kansas, 77; Collegiate Vet-
    erans Association, 75
University of Minnesota, 45, 47, 48
University of Nevada, Las Vegas, 77
University of North Carolina System, 55,
    56; General Administration, 57
University of Pittsburgh, 74–78
University of West Florida (UWF),
    61–68; academic programs to enhance
    success of military students at, 64–65;
    Academic Technology Center, 64;
    connections, partnerships, opportuni-
    ties, and programs to enhance success
    for military students at, 61–68; Coun-
    seling Center, 66; Hometown Heroes
    Teach, 64–65; Military Appreciation
    Day, 65; Military Connections Com-
    mittee, 65, 66; and military personnel
    as students in higher education,
    62–63; and national and campus orga-
    nizations facilitating collaborations at,
    63–64; President's Military Commu-
    nity Advisory Council, 61, 63, 64; rec-
    ommendations on how to enhance

success of military students at, 66–68; Student Disability Resource Center (SDRC), 66; student services and support programs to assist military learners at, 65–66; Veteran's Services Office, 65, 66; Vocational Rehabilitation, 66; war affects on campus life at, 62

Urasano, R. J., 46

U.S. Air Force, 62

U.S. Army, 46, 85; 1/34 Brigade Combat Team (BCT), 46, 47

U.S. Army National Guard, 27

U.S. Department of Defense, 36–38, 62, 64, 84, 90, 91; Task Force on Mental Health, 46; Tuition Assistance program, 90

U.S. Department of Defense Mental Health Advisory Committee, 13

U.S. Department of Defense Task Force on Mental Health, 13, 36–37

U.S. Department of Education, 56, 90

U.S. Department of Justice, 91

U.S. Department of Labor, 91

U.S. Department of Veterans Affairs, 35, 37, 50, 57, 62, 65, 76, 82, 89, 91, 92

U.S. House of Representatives Committee on Veterans' Affairs, 92, 93

U.S. Marine Corps, 46, 85, 86

U.S. Navy, 64

USERA. See Public Law 103–353); Uniformed Services Employment and Reemployment Rights Act (USERRA

UWF. See University of West Florida (UWF)

VA. See Veterans Administration (VA)

Veteran-friendly, 45

Veteran-friendly campuses, statewide approach to creating: and higher education initiative in Minnesota, 46–47; and Minnesota Department of Veterans Affairs-Higher Education Veterans Programs, 48–49; and Minnesota's legislative efforts in 2006, 47–48; and Minnesota's legislative efforts in 2007, 48; overview of, 45–46; and St. Cloud State University Veterans Organization, 52; and St. Cloud State University Veterans Services, 49–52; summary, 53

Veterans Administration (VA), 8, 9, 30, 32, 37, 50, 66, 84, 92

Veterans of Foreign Wars (VFW), 32, 51, 52, 67–68

VFW. See Veterans of Foreign Wars (VFW)

Vietnam conflict, 26, 27, 29, 31, 35, 72, 81

Vietnam veterans, 16, 71

Vietnam Veterans Against the War, 72

Vogt, D., 38

Wain, H. J., 46

Walter Reed Army Medical Center, 82, 83, 85

Walton County, Florida, 63–64

Wan, W., 28

War on Terror, 28

War Trash (Jin), 31

Washington, D.C., 83

Washton, N. S., 29

Waterhouse, M., 15

Waters, E. B., 12

Whitt, E. J., 13

Wiley, L., 61

Wilson, A. T., 37

Winn, B. A., 16

Wisconsin Department of Veterans Affairs, 46

Women veterans, meeting needs of: and mental health problems, 35–36; need for further research on, 42; overview, 35–36; and post-traumatic stress disorder, 35–36; and sexual assault, 37–38; suggestions for practitioners on, 41; and understanding identity development of women veterans, 38–40

Workforce Development Board (Florida), 64–65

Workforce Escarosa (Florida), 64–65

World War I, 26

World War II, 26, 29, 46, 71, 90

Yankelovich, Inc., 930

Zoroya, G., 82